Wake Up and Roar

Papaji H.W.L Poonja

EasyRead Large

Copyright Page from the Original Book

Sounds True, Inc.
Boulder, CO 80306

© 2007 Eli Jaxon-Bear

SOUNDS TRUE is a trademark of Sounds True, Inc.
All rights reserved. Published 2007.

Book design by Karen Polaski

No part of this book may be used or reproduced in any manner without written permission of the author and publisher.

ISBN 978-1-59179-589-6

Library of Congress Cataloging-in-Publication Data

Poonja, H. W. L.
  Wake up and roar / H. W. L. Poonja. — 2nd ed.
    p. cm.
  Originally published: Kula Maui, HI : Pacific Center Pub., 1992.
  ISBN 978-1-59179-589-6 (hardcover)
  1. Spiritual life—Hinduism. 2. Hinduism—Doctrines. I. Title.

BL1237.36.P66 2007
294.5'44—dc22

2007002230

Digital Edition 12/09
ISBN: 978-1-59179-885-9 (digital)

TABLE OF CONTENTS

FOREWORD	v
ABOUT SRI POONJAJI	xv
THE CRY OF FREEDOM	1
PURIFICATION	10
WHO ARE YOU?	11
DOUBT, FEAR, AND IMPEDIMENTS	26
MIND AND KILLING THE EGO	56
THINKING AND EMPTINESS	64
PRACTICE AND MEDITATION	82
WHAT TO DO	104
THE VEHICLE TO LIBERATION	122
CHOOSING SAMSARA OR NIRVANA	128
LEELA	137
DESIRE	149
REALIZATION	167
THE GURU	176
WHAT IS ENLIGHTENMENT?	190
REQUIREMENTS FOR SATSANG	202
RELATIONSHIP TO THE TEACHER	211
THE NATURE OF I	228
MEDITATION	250
THE NATURE OF MIND AND VASANAS	280
TRAP OF THE SENSES	316
INQUIRY AND DEVOTION	348
CHOOSING TOTAL DEATH	383
HOW TO BE IN THE WORLD	400
THE ROMANCE OF LOVE: THE HIDDEN SECRET	423
GLOSSARY	433
ABOUT THE EDITOR	436

ABOUT SOUNDS TRUE	438
FRONT COVER FLAP	439
BACK COVER FLAP	441
BACK COVER MATERIAL	442

Image A

Image B: Sri Ramana Maharshi

Image C: H.W.L. Poonja

*In this play of Kali Yuga
Sri Ramana established
Silence and Self-inquiry
In the sattvic realm.
For this he is called Maharishi.*

*Sri Poonjaji tossed the flame
Of silence
Into the marketplace.
He set the secret burning of
non-abidance
Loose in the land of activity.
And the world is catching fire.
For this he is called Papaji,
Beloved father of all.*

—A DEVOTED SON
ELI JAXON-BEAR

FOREWORD

I first knocked on Papaji's door in Hardiwar, India, in 1990. Opening the door himself, he greeted us with a huge smile and flashing eyes. He opened his arms uninhibitedly and, nearly shouting, he cried out, "Welcome!" Over the days and weeks to come, I watched him offer this same welcome to whoever appeared at his door for satsang.

Typically, we would spend the days sitting quietly with him in his room on the banks of the Ganga [Ganges]. Sometimes a visitor would ask a question regarding the search for truth. Always, Papaji would cut to the heart of the question, and always in a way the questioner could most likely understand. With Buddhists, he would use the life or teachings of the Buddha to direct the questioner into a fresh, unique way of self-discovery. With Sufis, he might quote Kabir. With those of no religion or spiritual practice, he would speak unencumbered by religion or practice.

He enjoyed going over a visitor's travel plans or the train schedule for various points in India. No particular formula was needed to receive the direct transmission of truth that his presence freely offered to all. This, for me, created an atmosphere of relaxation, a letting go in my own mind of any concepts of what I should be learning, how I should be acting, or what my experience should be.

Occasionally, he would go around the room asking for reports of what had been realized. It was often at this point, through Papaji's confirmation and confidence in the questioner's realization, that one or more people in the room would internally catch fire with the all-inclusive expansiveness of consciousness consciously aware of itself. What tears and laughter of pure joy! How contagious it was! One person's awakening was everyone's awakening. Whether that awakening lasted a minute or a lifetime, what was directly experienced was one Self.

Sometimes, after being in this precious room together, we would have tea, or go for a walk, or visit the local market for vegetables and trinkets. On one such outing, I began to long for the atmosphere of his room, where grace and love were so obvious. Just as I began to follow my thoughts into sentimentality, he caught my eye, and his glance stopped me. What I received from that glance was the certain understanding that here, wherever one might be, is the same grace and love as in any holy meeting, on any mountaintop, or in any cave. Nothing can take it away, as everything, everything, exists only by that grace.

Shortly after Papaji's death on September 6, 1997, I received a phone call from one of the students who was with him until the end. This is what was reported:

In Papaji's last days, he fell ill with what was thought to be bronchitis. At a certain point he was taken to the hospital and put on a respirator, yet after a short time his heart also began to fail.

One of Papaji's closest students tried to question him as to what the procedure should be: should they continue allowing the doctors to work at life support, or should they stop? Instead of answering the question, Papaji somehow rallied out of a semiconscious state, and to the three people in the room gave his last teaching, literally only hours before his body was finished.

"He looked at one student and strongly, intensely, and fiercely asked, Where is the Buddha?"

The student was deeply struck by the question and instantly understood. Papaji saw this, and so he looked to the next and said, "Where is the Buddha?"

At first she replied, "You are the Buddha, Papaji."

Again, he demanded, "Where is the Buddha!"

Another person brought him a picture of Ramana and said, "Papaji, here is the Buddha."

With the same intensity, Papaji directed his question to each person in the room: "Where is the Buddha!"

He was heavily sedated, and again he slipped into a semiconscious state. His students were still very concerned as to what Papaji's wishes were for his body. Again they asked him, "Papaji, these doctors have many procedures that they can use to keep your body alive, but we have to know what it is you really want."

By some miracle of life force, in his severely weakened state Papaji put his arm around a student, grabbed his other hand, and, squeezing it very tightly, said, "Bas."

Bas, in Hindi, means "enough."

Again Papaji said, "Bas."

The students felt the deep satisfaction of knowing what Papaji wanted, and they all agreed among themselves, but the doctors had their own regulations and so continued to try to keep his body alive.

Papaji's heart stopped several more times and each time the doctors brought him back.

Finally, in much distress, his students urgently asked one another what could be done, how they might be able to intervene. One of them finally said, "Don't worry, Papaji will figure something out."

Shortly thereafter, a blockage developed in the intravenous line delivering Papaji's heart medicine, and the heart rhythm shifted radically. The doctors finally admitted that they could do nothing more, and Papaji left his body.

Those closest to Papaji reported that to be in his presence those last days was to be in the presence of pure peace and bliss. There was absolutely no suffering.

As is the Indian tradition, Papaji's body was burned in one of the burning ghats [funeral grounds] where he resided in the city of Lucknow, Uttar Pradesh. A few days later, his ashes were offered to his beloved river Ganga, in Haridwar, near Rishikesh.

Papaji's last teaching was also his first teaching. The root of his teaching, throughout all of his time with us, revolved around this type of inquiry: Where is Buddha? Where is awakened mind? You could also substitute the words "peace," "God," or "truth." Where is peace? Where is truth? Where is God? Finally, where is life itself? Where is life to be found?

Where do we look for truth, for God, for ourselves, for life? To receive the answer to these questions, we must first ruthlessly tell the truth about what has been found in those places where we have continued to look. Only then can we inquire of ourselves deeply, honestly, and ruthlessly: Where am I? Who am I?

I was profoundly sad at the loss of Papaji's form, yet I remain exquisitely joyful in the realization that what Papaji is can never be lost. It cannot shift with the dissolution of form. How is it possible that both are included? Because Papaji is life, and everything is included in life. What Papaji's form always relentlessly pointed to was that which was here before he was born, that which remains after he is gone, and that who he is, unborn and not subject to death, never separate from who you are, or from anything at all.

The ruthless message of Papaji's life and Papaji's death is to face the inevitable ending of all form, including one's own. It is the invitation to discover for oneself, without a doubt, that the truth of who one is formless presence of being. Not the body or the personality, not the thoughts or the emotions, not the personal history, but the discovery of oneself as the living truth of consciousness itself.

Living truth was the strength of Papaji's being and his living example, as well as his first and final teaching. Even though by all accounts he was paralyzed, some force came through him, and he demanded of those around him, "Where is Buddha?" He would not be satisfied until he saw the awakening and the realization of where Buddha truly is.

When I first heard of Papaji's last miraculous rallying, that his last words were a teaching, I was freshly overcome with gratitude for this brilliant force of nature called Papaji.

Someone once asked me what my life was like before I met Papaji, and I said, "Before Papaji, I didn't have a life; I had a story of suffering. But in the meeting of Papaji, I have only life; I am only life."

In meeting this huge force that has the potential to stop the suffering of one's life, there is a recognition of what is alive, the living truth. Not abstractly, not theoretically, not in some hypothetical past or future, but the living truth, as it always exists, alive and present in the core of all being.

Papaji began teaching when he was a young boy. People somehow found their way to him, and he had no idea what he was supposed to say. Yet he taught until his last breath, and always his teaching was pointing us within to what is beyond any idea of inside or outside ourselves.

Papaji's direct teaching was always to "see the seer." When this is seen, then wherever you are you will continue the gift that is Papaji.

If you feel a connection to Papaji, from having either met him, or heard about him, or read about him, or even from seeing a picture of him, I encourage you to open your mind as you read this book so that you can recognize what is already alive and present in the core of your own being.

This profound message, from this profound master, that somehow attracts you is yours already if you will have it. Papaji's body is gone, but his teaching is alive within each of us. If his teaching pierces your heart open, it will relentlessly reveal your true identity to be life itself.

Gangaji
Ashland, Oregon, 2006

ABOUT SRI POONJAJI

Sri Harilal W. Poonja was born on October 13, 1910, in Gujranwala, India. He spent his childhood in Lyalpur (now called Faisalabad). This is in the western part of the state of Punjab, which later became part of Pakistan. He was born to the sister of one of India's celebrated saints, Swami Ram Tirtha.

Ram Tirtha's poetry was rooted in the non-dual awareness that is the promise of Advaita Hinduism. His cadences, insights, and love of nature are remarkably echoed in the awakening of his nephew. Ram Tirtha went into seclusion in his beloved Himalayas and, in October 1906, at the age of thirty-four, walked into a raging river, never to return. A mural of Ram Tirtha on a wall of a temple in Rishikesh is so strikingly like a portrait of a young Poonjaji that the onlooker's breath is taken away. Sri Poonjaji was born in October four years later.

As a child, Harilal heard a radio broadcast from Peshawar about the Buddha. He became deeply inspired and felt he must surpass the Buddha, although he wasn't sure exactly what that meant.

Around this time, he saw a picture of the Buddha as a bony ascetic in a schoolbook. He began to secretly feed his food to the animals. Soon his ribs began to show.

He was very happy when his schoolmates would point and laugh and call, "Buddha, Buddha." His father, however, was not so pleased. Worried about his son's health, he took Harilal to the doctor, who got the young boy back on food.

Harilal still secretly dressed as a sadhu [renunciate] and went through town with a begging bowl, where he preached in the town square. While in high school and on the wrestling team, he read an article in a magazine about yoga. He changed his diet to only buffalo milk for a year as he practiced yoga.

His first deep samadhi [state of bliss] occurred around the age of nine, at the conclusion of the First World War. To celebrate the British victory samadhi [state of bliss] the children were given lapel pins and a holiday. The family was at a restaurant drinking mango shakes. When his drink was passed to him, Poonjaji did not respond. He was deeply absorbed and unaware of his surroundings. He was taken to a local mosque, where it was pronounced that he was possessed and mantras were recited.

Upon his returning to normal consciousness, his mother asked why he was laughing and crying all night. He could not say. She asked if he had seen Krishna. But he had not seen anything at all that could be named. He had no way of speaking about this experience. Soon, through his mother's strong influence, he became a devotee of Krishna, pursuing a mantra practice day and night that continued well after meeting his master in 1942.

When Poonjaji was twenty, his parents arranged his marriage and he entered the army as an officer. While in the army, his attendant was told, "Cut back on Poonja's whiskey ration." His servant replied that Poonja did not drink at all.

Instead, he arose at 2a.m. and began his devotional mantras, calling for a visit from Krishna. He now laughs that sometimes he even dressed in women's clothes to lure Krishna, who is famous for keeping the company of young women. It was the resulting bliss that was mistaken for drunkenness.

Although he was part of the bright, up-and-coming officers' group that was destined to take charge when the British left India, Poonjaji could not stay in his career. His heart's longing pulled him, and he re-signed his commission. Moving his family into his father's house and begging his father's support, he set off on his spiritual quest.

He ranged through much of India and up into the Himalayas, visiting monasteries, ashrams, and holy men. He was looking for God. He offered everything to anyone who could show him God. Everywhere he went he was disappointed, finding only "businessmen disguised as sadhus."

He was penniless and living at his father's house with his wife and two children when finally his master called him home. The story is a famous one.

It is recounted in Poonjaji's own words, in these pages. Appearing as a sadhu, the great maharishi Bhagavan Sri Ramana appeared at Poonjaji's home and directed him to go to Tiruvannamalai. There, at the feet of his master, his search ended.

For the next five years Poonjaji worked in Madras and spent all his spare time in the presence of his master. In 1947, someone pointed out to the maharishi that Poonjaji had family in the Muslim half of the Punjab. Bhagavan sent Poonjaji to rescue his family from the massacres that accompanied the partition of India. Poonjaji did not want to leave.

"All of that is a dream," he told his master. "I don't want to leave you."

"If it is a dream, what can the harm be?" the maharishi replied. "I will never leave you."

This truth was vividly demonstrated shortly thereafter.

While boarding the train from Lahore to Faisalabad, Poonjaji sensed Ramana's guidance, and instead of sitting in the car with the Hindus, he inexplicably boarded the car filled with Muslims.

Shortly after leaving the station, the Muslims stopped the train, and before Poonjaji's eyes they slaughtered all the Hindus.

While he tried to cover his tattoo of "Om" on his hand, he still had all the markings of a Hindu Brahmin, including his pierced ears. He continued the journey for another twenty hours, sitting unnoticed in the midst of the Muslims.

When he arrived in Faisalabad the situation was quite bad, with rioting in the streets. He managed to get thirty-five members of his family out on the last train leaving Lahore. The tracks were pulled up behind the train as it left.

Because he knew an army officer in Lucknow who could help him, Poonjaji moved his family there. His family has lived in Lucknow since then. (Remarkably, this is where Swami Ram Tirtha had, and still has, his Pratisthan.) He worked for a while in Lucknow for Allis-Chalmers, selling heavy earth-moving equipment.

Though he dutifully worked to provide for his family and his children's education, Poonjaji could not bear family life. After a few years he left his family in Lucknow and returned to the south, where he found a job as a mining engineer in the jungle of Mangalore. He lived in a simple hut in the forest, while supervising and being responsible for the lives of hundreds of men. He explored for new ore deposits in the jungle, visited Ramanashram, and had the occasional student find him.

One day the chief justice of India's Supreme Court heard of this God-intoxicated sadhu living in the jungle and went to find him. The justice was expecting to find a sadhu in a loincloth, and was very surprised to see Poonjaji in his leather boots and jacket, driving a jeep. However, with one look and a few words, the chief justice was singing and dancing in circles.

During a celebration of Guru Purnima, Poonjaji was passing unnoticed through a village. He stopped at a house for help and was invited in. Despite his muddy clothes and protestations to the contrary, they sat him in the place of the guru and worshipped him. They later built a small hut for him in the hope that he would return to the village. The wife of this couple, still alive at this writing, claims to be Poonjaji's oldest disciple. Her children, now in their forties, are his disciples as well.

As soon as his children were grown, educated, and married, Poonjaji retired. In 1966 he began traveling throughout India, spreading the realization that had consumed him. He lived in a cave on the banks of the Ganga, cooking over a fire and eating off a flat rock.

During the Kumba Mela, a massive religious festival that happens once every twelve years, millions come to bathe in the Ganga and receive her darshan. At a Maha Kumba Mela, which happens after twelve kumbas, or 144 years, Poonjaji had a remarkable vision. Further up the bank and away from the crowds, he saw a beautiful young woman with eyes he had never seen on a human. She approached him and he asked where her parents were. She said she was there to take darshan from him. She prostrated at his feet, then walked into the river and disappeared. It was only then that he realized he had met Ganga, the spirit of the river.

At one point Poonjaji went off in search of the hidden rishis that are reputed to be immortal soma-eaters, hidden in the recesses of the Himalayas. While journeying far back in the mountains, he met a Kashmiri siddha yogi. They agreed to share what they had realized. The yogi displayed his powers. The man could levitate, and had been given a staff by Yama, the Lord of Death. He told Poonjaji that as long as he had this staff, he would not die.

When the siddha invoked the goddess Saraswati, he could speak in languages he had never learned. Poonjaji, capable in Persian, English, Tamil, and several other south Indian languages, tested the man to his satisfaction.

The man said that his master had taught him everything he knew. But his master had also told him that this was not ultimate knowledge. On his deathbed, his master sent him out to find ultimate knowledge.

After this display, the yogi asked if Poonjaji could help him find ultimate knowledge. Poonjaji agreed. First, he took the man's staff and threw it into the Ganga.

"Now," Poonjaji said, "this body will live and die like everyone else. All you have shown me has been done with mind power. Mantras, the appearance of gods and powers—all are done with mind and body. Now, stop for a minute..."

Poonjaji looked into the man's eyes. "Now try," Poonjaji said. "Invoke your gods and see what happens."

Nothing happened. With a quiet mind, the man could not use his powers. Then, with a word, Poonjaji enlightened him with ultimate knowledge.

The siddha prostrated at Poonjaji's feet. He said, "My master told me, 'If you ever find anyone who gives you this knowledge, you must serve him for the rest of your life.' So, sir, I am your servant. I will go with you."

Poonjaji told the man that he always traveled alone. He did not let him stay.

In the late 1960s, Poonjaji was discovered by many of the early hippie seekers. He was staying in a cave on the banks of the Ganga, and they would sneak away from their ashrams to come and be with him. He was impressed with their desire and commitment.

Many of these young seekers invited Poonjaji to come and teach in different parts of the world. He traveled throughout Europe, the United States, Australia, and South America. Wherever he went, he allowed no ashram, no organization, and he refused to settle down.

"The whole universe is my ashram," he explained.

This book is based on tape-recorded satsangs that occurred in Lucknow and Hardiwar, India, between January 1990 and April 1991. The satsangs, which were open to everyone, took place in Sri H.W.L. Poonja's home. The voices and questions of the various participants are presented here as one voice.

1
THE CRY OF FREEDOM

There is a river of thought-waves. Everyone is being washed downstream. Everyone is clinging to these thoughts and being washed away.

Just give rise to the single thought "I want to be free." This thought will rarely come out of the entire population. The entire population of the planet is moving downstream. They are not destined to give rise to the thought "I want to be enlightened in this very span of time."

So I call this thought of freedom going against the stream and toward the source. It does not require any effort to give rise to this thought. The thought "I want to be free" is itself free. This thought will take you to freedom. It is the most rare thought. Out of the entire population of six billion, only a handful give rise to this thought.

2

Master, I have been with you for four days now, and I am still not enlightened.

[*laughing*] Yes, I am surprised, a smart boy like you.

What should I do?

Let me tell you what my teacher told me. Just be quiet. This quiet does not involve talking or not talking. It does not involve any doing whatsoever. Just let the mind fall into silence. This is enough.

Now wait. I can't believe what you just said to him. I've been trained to think that it takes years and years of practice and lifetimes of training and hard work to reach liberation. Now you say it's simply a switch on the wall, a change of perception. Is that correct?

You need not switch on or off. For the sun to shine do you switch it on?

No.

Just like this. This light is always there. No switches at all. The sun has no switches. You turn your face away and you call it night. Sun has no night and no day. You are that sun. This is your own light and you are that. You don't need any switches. The switches are limitations. You have fixed these limitations yourself. Nature has not fixed any switches.

"I want this, I want that. I dislike this, I like that." If you remove this switch of like and dislike, how will you feel? Instantly you will be free. Likes and dislikes keep you in bondage and suffering.

There are no walls for the switches either. Walls are imaginary only, like walls between countries. You have constructed this wall between you and something else. You have to break this which does not exist.

The frontier you have created is the suffering. You have to demolish it by yourself. Nobody will help you.

What do you mean, "Nobody will help you"?

The Self has to help the Self; nobody else can help. Who else will drop this wall? You have to help yourself. Find out, is it possible to be out of the Self, ever?

First say, "I want help." Then discover who needs help. Self is not suffering. Self is not in bondage. Self is ever free.

So you are saying it is the mind clinging to the wall that is suffering?

Yes. Who has created separation? Mind has created separation, and no mind will remove this separation. The separation doesn't exist. Even to say "I am separate" is a joke.

It is only when there is a need for understanding that there is something to be understood. Once some of Krishnamurti's students came here to see me. They said there is only one difference between our teachings. They said, "Krishnamurti removes concepts from the vessel and Poonjaji breaks the vessel altogether." [*laughs*]

So allow yourself some time, a couple of moments. And in those moments there should be no trespassing. Make available a few seconds, and during this span nobody should trespass. I think you could well afford to be available for a few moments. You have spent all your life for others, and not even a minute for your Self.

Everyone possesses you. When you are born, your parents say you are "my son." Go to school next and you're "my student." Then marry and you're "my husband." Have children and you're "my father." Remove these possessions. Let no one possess you. Reject everything and see what happens.

You have to devote some time for your Self, either now or in some other lifetime. You have to reach your home. There is no escape. You have to return home, either now or tomorrow. You must decide if you want to play more. It doesn't matter. In the end, it doesn't matter.

You think it is taking time. It is no time that you are spending because you are already free; it is only your illusion that you are not. You have to allow time, once and for all, if you want to be happy. The moment you declare "I am free!"—standing on the mountaintop of your toes, arms up—eureka! There is the happy moment. Very happy moment.

***

What prevents you from freedom? What is the impediment?

That I often have lots of thoughts and it is very difficult to get rid of them.

What kind of thoughts do you have? Do you give rise to the thought of freedom?

Yes.

Hold on to this thought of freedom. Do you see any other thoughts simultaneously rising up?

No.

Mind can hold on to only one thought at a time.

I understand.

Tell which other thoughts replace this thought of freedom. Voluntarily bring another thought to replace this. Another thought that you like best. Do it ... do it!

I don't want to reject this thought.

Very good. Very nice. When you like this thought, where will this thought take you? Where will other thoughts be? Where is freedom? How many kilometers away from you?

I don't think it is far away from me.

If it is not far from you, then how much time is needed for you to arrive here? How much time to be as you are?

It is here and now. How much time to be here and now?

As little as possible.

Let us agree, as little as possible. Should we call it this moment? This instant? The least possible time. This instant is the time. Now look at this moment, the least time. Look into this instant, if it is not far away. Jump into it right now.

How?

Now! [*much laughter*] Now, what is the thought now?

None. Only this now.

No thoughts troubling you now?

Only that I am looking for thoughts.

Yes, yes. Keep on looking for thoughts. Do you understand what you are saying?

Yes.

If you don't look for a thought, the thoughts will look for you. If you don't look, all the thoughts will attack you. Try. If you look for a thought, do you catch it?

They have disappeared.

Then when the thoughts have disappeared, who are you? [*silence*]

This is the best answer you can give me. Stay as such. If you step out of the silence, there is trouble. You don't need anything. Eternity is here. Happiness is here. No death can enter this silence. No trouble can enter here. Step out and there is samsara—the endless cycle of birth and death. No thought, no concept, can enter here. All desires are met here in emptiness. You walk out chasing after desires and they are never fulfilled.

***

All my life, even as a little boy, the desire for freedom has been stronger than all other desires. It doesn't really seem to be a desire; it's more like a longing. This desire seems to pull me back, while the other desires seem to pull me out. This desire for freedom mysteriously seems to stay, where the other desires come and go and change with my thoughts. The desire for freedom is always there, burning. It seems to be deeper than the mind. Is this true?

This is the most intense desire. All other desires are on the surface. They rise and fall, you see. The desire for freedom is intense and you must respond to it. When you respond, this desire will bring you back home. It will continue to trouble you if it is not fulfilled in this life span.

This desire must be fulfilled, whether you like it or not. That is why you come here. What a farce! This desire follows you wherever you go, in whatever incarnation you take. It will not leave you. How did it push you here? You left your job and your business; why did you have to come here? Just consider it. You must return home! How long can you stay at the market?

It seems the only response to the desire is to look within to where the mind originates. To go to the place where thoughts arise and stay with it. That is the response, isn't it?

Yes. You will unceasingly scan the mind. Unceasingly. And you will know who you are.

PURIFICATION

When I think of the notion of purification it seems absolutely ridiculous. I wonder if you would speak about the value of purification. Many teachers tell their students to do more purification so that their realization is more powerful.

First of all, [if you are] to purify yourself, there must be some dust inside the teacher's mind and he wants someone to wipe it out. There is, in truth, no dust at all. It is a waste of time to purify what is not dusty. From where has the dust accumulated? And where will you move this dust to; where will you throw it? With which broomstick will you do it? If you look, there is no place for dust to alight. Better to dust out the concept of purification. You are that emptiness itself. Where can dust alight?

WHO ARE YOU?

A new visitor was asked this question:

Who are you? I'll give you five minutes because you are Indian. These others may think I treat you better because you are Indian and they are all foreigners. So I will. I will give you five minutes for this question.

Five minutes! I have been working on this question for two and a half years!

You are right. Five minutes is too long, but you are a guest. I want to treat you well.

Look, how far is it from Kanpur, where you came from, to here?

About ninety kilometers, about three hours.

Three hours. Now, why does it take three hours?

Because of the distance.

Very good, very good. So where is the *I* that is asking the question? And where is the *I* in "Who am I?" I gave you five minutes to be polite. But if

there is no space—no distance—your answer should take no time!
***

I was very touched yesterday when you spoke of obedience. Living obedience every second, obedience to that every second.

Yes.

Obedience implies a duality, doesn't it?

It is your own Self. Where is the duality?

Only Self.

You love your Self. Is it not obedience?

The river merging, the river discharging into the sea—is it not obedience? Externally, you can call it obedience, going back to meet herself. You can call it obedience, or you can call it return to the source, according to your temperament. And the ocean is happy to receive you.

If obedience is given to anyone else, then you call it duality. But where is duality? You have two hands, two feet, ten fingers, a nose ... how many parts to this body, but when you say "I," is it duality?

When you see your face in the mirror, are there two persons? When you see truth, you know there has never been duality. Right from the beginning until the end of the universe.

I was thinking of the Self creating multiplicity for its own enjoyment.

When you cross the ocean, you will see the emptiness of unity. When you dream, you see many different people, of many different ages, and you see mountains that are millions of years old and different stars or whatever. And when you are awake, was what you saw in the dream unity or multiplicity?

A dream within the unity.

When you wake up, unity also goes. Duality goes also. So when you wake up from this waking sleep, you return to emptiness. Whenever we see objects, we are dreaming. And when we are dreaming, this means we are also sleeping. So you have to wake up with a shout: "I want to be free!" With this shout, you will wake up and everything goes. Otherwise, you will be reborn again and again in endless cycles of kalpas [4,320,000,000 years: Brahmic cycle for the end of the universe].

***

Is enlightenment or Self-realization just an awareness, a self-evident awareness of Being?

Yes, it is awareness. Total awareness or Being, same thing. No difference. Total awareness. Everything is there. And you are that awareness.

I have this awareness. Yet, as everybody knows, your realization is much deeper than mine. What is the difference?

You make a difference. Otherwise, there is no difference.

If I were to sit there, where you are, after one week nobody would come here anymore.

You can try. Come here. [*everyone laughs*] When I asked the difference, my master removed my difference and I accepted it.

Maybe that is the point. I do not accept enough. But I have it.

Do not accept enough? [*laughs*] I accepted it and then there was no problem. If you accept, there will be no problem. If you accept "I am free," then you are free. If you accept "I am not free," you are not free.

***

Yesterday you said everyone must one day face the truth. If I freely believe, then am I enlightened?

No! *I am* does not need your belief or disbelief! From the *I am* there is no difference. Fully accept *I am,* that's all. If you have some grades of acceptance, that is, "Slowly I will try to accept; I will practice to accept," then you will slowly accept. It depends on you. It will not change.

Enlightenment will not change today, tomorrow, the next day. It is the same. Get it now, or after one year, or in this life span. It will not change.

You are not accepting it. Accept it fully, and where is the problem? You are already free. Who tells you that you are not free? You are not opening to it. You are afraid to even utter "I am free." I do not know what that fear is.

When people say, "I am bound, I am suffering, I am miserable," they feel free to speak. "I am free! I am deathless!" nobody speaks. Whose fault is this? Whatever you say, whatever you think, is going to happen. It will be fulfilled, now or tomorrow. If you think "I am free," then you are free.

People don't fully desire freedom. How many people desire freedom? I tell you that you are already free and you don't accept it. You want to do something. Freedom doesn't need any effort. Other things may need effort. Freedom is free. Free of your efforts.

So no more struggle, just accept it.

Then it will be there. When you don't make any effort, it is there. When you try to catch it, it goes further away, because you are making an effort for the thing that is already there.

That is what I have learned from you. I am so thankful.

[*laughs*] Very nice. You learned it here, then your work is finished. If you don't make any effort whatsoever, you are That Itself.

***

This desire for freedom and the thought "Who am I?"—are they the same?

Same. Same. "Who am I?" brings you back if you have the desire for freedom. To whom did this desire arise? "To me," you say. Then find out who you are.

Freedom is faith in the present moment?

Why faith in the present? In the present moment, who is there to have faith in whom? In the present, to have faith is always something of the past. How can you have faith in the present moment? When the word "faith" comes, it takes you to the past.

I wanted to say that faith means to see that there is nothing else but the present moment.

Yes. That's right. The present moment is freedom. Look into the present moment. Freedom itself. You are always looking into the past moments. When did you give occasion to the present moment to manifest? You have never given a chance to this present moment. Always you are related to the past only. You are not giving your thought to this instant. This instant is the present moment. Look into it. Then you will see your face.

When you use this word "I," then stop and look where this *I* arises from. This is the present moment. Look at this *I* and you will know this present moment, and then what is your faith? Where does it arise from? If you go forward, you will go to the past. Return back to this, to where the thought *I* arose from. Return back from whatever place to there.

***

You are free always! You don't have to run anywhere for freedom. You have to run for something else. Where is freedom, enlightenment, peace, bliss? It is here. Now, to be here, what effort is needed? You do not have to do anything to stay as you are.

Where can you turn? You only have to turn when you are somewhere else. To turn from where? When you are at home, no flight is needed. Just remove these wrong ideas that you have borrowed from someone else, from society, your parents, your religion. It is not your nature to be unhappy or to suffer.

Does it go quickly or slowly, slowly?

Slowly is only the mind that fools you. To be right now, what understanding is needed? To be right now what you already are, you don't need any understanding or misunderstanding.

Why did I come here then?

You came here because you thought you were there!

***

When I look in your eyes, I see just Self. And I realize that when I honor you, I am honoring Self. But I still haven't learned to honor the Self in everyone. I can honor it in you, but I still make comparisons and judgments of others. I don't see the Self in everyone.

First you have to see the Self within you! Then within me, and then everywhere else.

But when I look in other people's eyes, I can't see it so clearly.

First see the Self within you. Then you will see that the Self in you is not other than the Self in me; it is the same Self. Then you perceive that the same Self in you, in me, is everywhere else. And Self alone is that Self. There is nothing apart from the Self. This experience you will surely get if you stick to Self alone. Nothing else ever existed at all!

But I—

Okay, let's tackle it another way. When you see the Self, don't see the "not-Self" at the same time. If you do not see the not-Self here and there and everywhere, what will you see?

Only the Self.

Only the Self everywhere! The not-Self doesn't exist. And the Self is not absent at all! So you will see Self everywhere. When I say everywhere, it is nowhere. Nowhere itself. Because no distance is involved. No here and somewhere. Self alone is total awareness of Self.

And all those waves and eddies and drops and bubbles—all are just the ocean. So, according to your question, "I see the ocean" is saying "I see the ocean within myself but not in the waves or other eddies, tides, bubbles. There I do not see." So you have to see first the ocean within the ocean, Self within the Self. And this will include everything else. You will contain everything.

The Self contains everything. There is nothing apart from it. This is why you can call it emptiness. There is nothing beyond emptiness. All is empty. Nothing ever exists.

And when you see something existing, it is not other than you. So wherever there is an idea or concept of duality, of something else, there is confusion there about this. There is no duality at all. Oneness and wholeness is all.

If we accept duality, then there must be frontiers between the two, and then it cannot be limitless. There will be a division between duality and union. So there cannot be any divisions or frontiers in limitless reality or in truth or emptiness. There are no frontiers. So this is seeing Self everywhere!

***

I have just come from a very busy culture and a very busy life in San Francisco—a life and culture filled with stress, noise, choices, confusion, and so much doing and activity. Suddenly I come here, and suddenly there is just Self. Everything turns back to the Self. It is so simple. I am struck by the simplicity of your guidance. Just immediately! So simple. Just paying attention to the Self. How will it be when I go back to San Francisco?

Simplicity will not be lost. You cannot lose simplicity. Simplicity is nature.

We forget that.

It will not forget you. You may forget her, but she will not forget you. She is very chaste.

I will try to remember that.

It is the easiest and simplest of everything that you do, even easier than breathing. Easier than the breath that you inhale or exhale. For here you are neither to inhale nor to exhale. Where does the inhalation and exhalation take place? You inhale, and it stops. You exhale, and it stops. And there, this is what you are. In between the inhaling and exhaling. Not even the effort to inhale or to exhale is needed.

Or from where does thought arise? There must be some activity for the thought to arise and go somewhere.

But the source doesn't go, doesn't come—it is as it is. How simple it is. [*much laughter*] I have to laugh sometimes because I see fish in the river crying, "I am thirsty." "I want enlightenment" is the same thing. [*more laughter*]

What is near and easy you don't pay any attention to. What is difficult and far—the moon, Mount Everest—you are attentive to. No one has arrived at the Self this way.

***

Who am I? Investigate it. Start with the question itself. First investigate *who*. Next investigate *am*. Next investigate *I*. When you return to the *I*, the question will disappear and no answer will be there.

That is your answer. That no answer is the answer. The river returns to the source from which it arises—the ocean—and disappears. No further inquiry to search for the river is needed. The river becomes the source.

We are all returning to the source. Every sentence that we speak returns. Every activity is moving toward itself.

You only have to be aware and your journey will be ended. We are in the source itself. Even if you don't try, you are already there. Make this choice. Choose "I am free," and you are free. Choose "I am bound," and you are bound.

It is your choice. You choose to be bound. You choose to suffer. So if you have the choice, choose happiness and freedom. Let it be a good choice of love.

When all other choices have failed miserably and the result is suffering, we have been cheated. So let us go the other way. Nothing known has ever given us lasting happiness so far. Anything known is not permanent. Anything that has name and form is not permanent. Let us try nameless and formless emptiness this time, in this blessed span of life.

***

I make it so complicated when I think, "What is the Self?" You make it sound so simple. You say, "I *am* the Self."

Yes. This simplicity is too difficult for you to digest.

I am looking for a concept of Self instead of "I *am* the Self."

You need not make any speculation or conceptualization. This is the doer itself and you have to agree. You cannot disagree. Can you speak to anyone else and say, "I am not Self?" And if you do, what will he think of you? [*laughs*]

When you are through the word "I," you are complete. *I* contains everything. It is sufficient. If you call yourself by the name "I," there will be no difficulty. You will be eternity. No death can touch you. Just remain *I.* That's all you have to do. How difficult is it? What is the difficulty in baptizing yourself "I am I"? That's all.

That simplifies it.

Too simple to accept?

DOUBT, FEAR, AND IMPEDIMENTS

This morning I was lying on my bed, and I had many doubts about what I am doing here and many, many thoughts. And suddenly I felt, "But what is this? I am lying on the bed and that is it." All the doubts suddenly went away and I felt very calm inside.

That is present moment. How long did you stay in present moment, and what did you do to lose it?

I tried to analyze what had happened.

Whatever is too near is difficult to attend to. The eyes see everything. But the eyes do not see themselves. Like this, the Self through the mind sees all the world, but the mind doesn't return back home to be the Self.

How do we overcome fear?

By giving up all practices in that direction.

At that moment when the fear is thick—[*snaps fingers*]—what do you do? At that moment between when you placed your fingers together and the snap, what did you do? Where did the sound of the snap come from?

This sound came from undoing it. Do it [*places fingers in position for snap*], then undo. All that you have done, heard, seen, and read—for a moment, forget about this and tell me, what is your face? What do you see? By simply undoing, what do you arrive at?

Nothing.

Ah. That is the return to your question: How to do? Undo, and where do you arrive? A distance between thought and thought. This dive is the same as nothingness. When you are absolutely happy, this is the same as nothingness.

When you are absolutely happy to meet your beloved after twenty years, what is the thought in your mind? No thought.

Surrounded by nothingness you have to do nothing. You have to do nothing to be who you are. Nothing at all.

To become something, of course, to become a doctor, is different. This is not a return to your true nature. You are always here. You deny it. You don't accept your greatness.

Being eternity itself, reality itself, how can you say, "I am suffering in this body"?

What can you do without *I*? Wherever you go, who is there? You can't lose this, even in suffering. "I suffer," you say. Try to leave. Breath in breath, who is more related to you?

***

I am feeling much fear and vulnerability. I understand that the world is a projection, yet I feel this fragmentation.

This fear is due to the first shock of wisdom, of light. It is as if this room was closed for the last twenty years, and you enter this dark room with a torch in hand to locate the light switch. This darkness has been established for twenty years. Instantly the light is there. The darkness is confused. Fear of disappearance is there.

After twenty years of darkness, how much time should it take when you face the light? What has happened? Fear in the mind of darkness. In an instant it cannot be there when you face the light. The darkness of the room does not go in installments. You think you have been here for twenty years in darkness. That fear is ingrained in you. You have been living for millions of years like this, millions of years.

This fear of facing the light is not a fear like other fears. This is a fear of eternity. Eternal ocean of nectar, and you are swimming holding on to darkness.

Somehow you get a push, or you intend to jump into the ocean of immortality yourself. In between leaving this place of darkness and the leap, fear arises.

Without touching the light and after leaving the darkness, neither can you turn back nor have you yet touched the surface. In this instant, there is what can be called fear. Fear to leap into eternity because "I will lose this body consciousness, this darkness." This is only the fear of facing the light. You will become nectar itself, no death at all.

***

I have an impediment. This impediment is a doubt, and it keeps me from loving you fully. It is giving me a headache.

What kind of headache do you have? There are two kinds that I know of. One is from carrying a load on your head. The other is from having the load removed. If you suddenly have no load on your head, this can seem disorienting; you lose your balance and have a headache. No load can also seem like a headache.

There was once a wealthy man who knew he was to die. He had never prepared himself spiritually, never meditated. So he hired twenty workers from the marketplace to meditate for him. He said, "I will give you double wages and feed you your meals."

The workers were very excited. They wanted to begin right away but did not know what to do. "Just sit like this," the man told them as he showed them the meditation posture.

After a few hours, the workers rebelled. "Keep your double wages," they said. "This will make us sick, sitting here doing nothing." And so they quit.

So I don't know what kind of headache you have, but I suggest you give up the very idea of impediment. This idea, in itself, is now the only impediment. The scriptures say there are certain impediments to give up. First is the idea of a personal identity, a personality, name and form, as to who you are. Give this up; detach from it.

Next is the idea of heaven after you die. The idea of merit and demerit, that action will get you anywhere. Give up this attachment as well.

And then God. Give up your attachment to God itself. The idea that there is some agency outside of yourself that can help you now. Give this up.

And then give up the very idea of giving up! This must also be abandoned!

Yesterday you said, "Tie up your camel and pray to Allah." I say now, ride your camel and forget about Allah! Ride the camel and you need not pray. If you tie it, you will have to untie it. If you tie it to a tree, you are also tied to it, so who will pray to Allah?

Impediment is only retaining the idea of impediment. The idea of the disappearance of impediment is the last impediment. This is the last hurdle, the last rung, the last leap forward.

Yes, there is a leap and there is the fear of emptiness—no name, no form. There is the fear of embracing this emptiness. You don't see anything there. Unknown! Absolutely empty! You need courage to hug that emptiness of no name and no form. Nobody can help you. Help can take you to the edge. But no one can help you here. The idea that there is help is itself an impediment. Throw away everything in name and form, and jump!

***

I always seem to give rise to more questions and doubts.

One day the king said to his minister, "Go out at dawn and find the first person that you meet, and I will give him a kingdom."

The minister went out at dawn and the first person he met was a beggar. He took this beggar to the palace and sat him on the throne. He was bathed and clothed and fed a royal feast. But soon the beggar asked, "Where is my begging bowl? It is time for me to beg."

While sitting on the throne, he still had the idea of a begging bowl. Who can help that beggar-king put down his begging bowl? Such is the case with you.

I get to the edge and my head tells the feet to jump, but my feet don't go. The courage doesn't get to the feet. Is there anything I could do, or not do, that might get the courage to the feet?

Neither! Neither doing nor not doing. Do not allow your mind to abide anywhere, not even in the nothingness.

***

What is it that takes birth then?

Unfulfilled samskaras [tendency, desire] take birth.

And the Self?

The Self is not touched. Only the body is born and dies. Your cumulative samskaras give rise to the impetus for another lifetime. This unceasing rebirth is called samsara. It is suffering. This goes on until enlightenment.

Enlightenment is the fire of knowledge which burns the samskaras, and then your birth and death problems end.

You say the body is like a dress?

Anything that you call "my"—such as "my body, my house, my car, my sweater, my wife." What is the difference? To whom does this body belong? Who is it that wears the body? My mind, my intellect, my memories, my dress—whose are they? Who are you to whom these things belong?

The body is different. The body is a part of you, whereas the car, the dress, the sweater are not.

Anything that is real must stay the same always. Now, for the dress—when you sleep, where is the dress and where is the body? When you sleep, who is present? The body is not there, nor the dress, nor the sweater. Who is it to whom all these belong? Ask yourself, "Who am I?" Then you will know what the body is, what the mind is, and what all these possessions are.

Well, I could just let it go—

No, no! I am not asking you to let go. I am asking you to see. If I say "your sweater" or "your pants," where does your mind cling? Where do you run to cling?

To the sweater.

Okay. Now ask, "Who am I?" Go and cling to *I* and then report what you are clinging to. "Who am I?" In this, *I* is an object. Let this object be clung to. Let your mind go toward the Self and cling and tell me what it is.

You are returning the thought to the place from where it arises. "My thought, my mind"—return these things to the place from where they spring forth. Return to the origin of the thought itself, and you will find *I*. Then we can speak of the body and mind, but first you must know who you are. Everything else will be easy after that.

First locate where you are, and then we can find the distance to where we have to proceed. Let us see where we are just now, on the map, and then we will see where we have to go. *I* is a place where you presently are, isn't it?

Yes.

So find out; let your thought go toward the *I* and see what happens.

Empty!

Ah. Right, right, very good answer. So *I* is empty. You send your mind to find the source of the *I,* the source of your being, the source of everything, and you said, "Empty."

Now, from this emptiness let us proceed. First you turned to face the light. You turned to face your Self. From there, from emptiness, now face the other side, the wrong side, where you see bodies, sweater, house, car, wife. You slowly step out of this emptiness and tell me what you see. You see it from emptiness now. What are you going to see?

Now.

Emptiness is always now, yes. Never then. So step out of this now. Proceed out of now and tell me where you go. Beyond this instant, what do you see?

[*long silence*] I feel thoughts coming up.

Let them come. Within emptiness, thoughts come. Within emptiness, what do they represent? Within the ocean, waves come. What do they represent? Within the emptiness, thoughts come. What do they represent?

The mind?

From the ocean waves arise, stay, move, and fall.

Still emptiness.

Good. All the waves that come from emptiness must be empty. Just as the waves that come from the ocean must be water only. They cannot be stones. Now, you bring a thought from emptiness which is not empty. Try it and investigate.

There is nothing there!

Very good. You have done the job. And that is your nature. This is what you are. You have to wake up. You are consciousness. You are empty. You are just in this moment only. Whenever you see name and form you are sleeping. What do you see in the world without name and form?

Where is consciousness as pure, immaculate eternity, permanent happiness, love, and bliss? When you look from there, from emptiness, you see everything. Nothing beyond that. Nothing to do. Only to be as you are.

We have misconceived ourselves that we have been born and we are the body and we are suffering and we have to die. Where it comes from, nobody knows; it is just a concept. It is not real. You have been trained by your family, your society, your religion. Yet this emptiness is your own nature. This is what you are, and really you need not do anything about it. You need not do penance or retire to a cave.

This is what you have to understand. I now answered your question from your own mind. If you see from emptiness, you will just see the waves of the ocean. And this is your projection. When you wake up and say "I am Ken," instantly there is samsara. Only your projection. When you don't give rise to a thought, you return to emptiness, to consciousness. When one thought arises, the world arises. One thought is the world.

And even this is just your projection and not other than you, as you are one. Just as your eyes, your ears, your hands are not apart from you.

This is how the world is. All the beings, the birds, the flowers, the rocks—all you, your Self. If somehow you understand it, where is the suffering? Suffering is always something else. Then only you suffer. When your total being is there and this total being is empty, then there will be no trouble.

So understand this, that this is who you are already. This is your own nature. You are that. You are already your own nature. You are that. You do not have to attain or acquire it.

We get preoccupied.

Yes. This preoccupation is death. If you know that all of this is me, then there will be no preoccupation and no past either. Do not fragment yourself into parts. Expand your understanding beyond limits. "I am so-and-so" is enough limitation to suffer.

Bondage arises only when you fragment yourself. You become the part and leave the rest and then try to understand. This is a drop of the ocean thinking, "I am separate from the ocean. I suffer and I must go on moving on the surface of the ocean. Always I am in fear of breakage, fear of a larger wave, so many fears."

There is no peace or safety in being free from the ocean or in running from the ocean. Not knowing that I am the same as the ocean creates confusion, suffering, and fear.

So long as we think, we will suffer. This samsara comes from one thought: "I am Ken." There is no difference between Ken and the whole of samsara. Can you separate Ken from samsara? When Ken proceeds to the source, then everything will be solved.

I find myself running away from myself. It becomes complicated. I forget.

Yes, yes. You forget. You only need your Self. Forget that you need a mirror. All that you see is only a reflection. When you remove this mirror, where does Ken disappear to?

Still here.

Yes. That mirror where you saw your face, remove it. That face is here. Reject this mirror. See who you are. Return to the place from where this thought arises.

Myself, emptiness, consciousness—same thing. You can't step out of it. It's always there. We only think it is not there; therefore, we search. Sometimes I am searching for glasses with which to read. Searching for the glasses while wearing them. I search everywhere and don't find them.

I see everything and don't find them. Through the glasses I am looking, because without the glasses I can't see, I can't search. Yet I can't see the glasses; I can't find them out there.

You are searching—"I want to be free." Through this thought you are searching for freedom. You will get it. This thought itself is the same as what you are searching for. This is consciousness! [*laughs*]

Where does consciousness go when I sleep?

How do you know it goes anywhere? When you wake up and you speak and then you sleep again, was this consciousness of sleep there or not? You say, "I had a very good sleep, no disturbance." Is it not consciousness when the body sleeps? Who is enjoying it? Consciousness of waking and consciousness of sleeping—no difference.

States pass in front of you as projected pictures pass across the screen. The screen is inactive and does not change. Whenever there is movement, there must be something that does not move. Identify yourself with the screen itself.

You are the screen, or the substratum, on which these states appear. And that is unseen. When you see something, the screen is not seen; when you see the screen, nothing is seen. When the screen is seen, the pictures are not seen.

When you are conscious, you don't see the projections of name and form. Wherever you see name and form, you don't see reality.

For example, there are several images made of gold. One image is of Christ, one is of a dog, and one is of a pig. Each is two hundred grams of gold. If you take one to a jeweler to melt it, which will fetch the best price? Pig, dog, or a god, same price. If you value the essence, same value. Essence is the same. If you remove name and form, nameless and formless, what are you? Who are you?

Are you saying gold is like the Self?

Yes, but because we are involved with name and form, we see the pig or the god. The moment we go back to the source and recognize the essence, the gold, the reality, the emptiness—this is nirvana! If we stay with the recognition of only the name and form—samsara! Reject the name and form, and immediately—nirvana.

***

What is karma?

I don't believe in karma. There is no past karma, no present karma, and no future karma. A man has three wives. One he is married to for ten years, one he is married to in the present, and another he will marry very soon.

Just before the last marriage, he dies. With his death, all three wives are widowed. With enlightenment, the same thing happens to the past, present, and future karmas.

If the doer is not there, the karmas are like widowed wives. His ego is dead now. This man who has no doubt has no karma. He has found liberation here and now. He is not born, not incarnated. It is what has been all the time; no changes have occurred.

The wives are widowed, and the liberated man is free and can do what he likes. It leaves no impression and so forms no karma.

Often, in the spiritual scene, this idea has led to permissiveness, license, harmfulness, and misunderstanding.

I am speaking of the non-doer. For the doer there will be a reaction and he will have to pay for it. One who is involved in attachments will reap the consequences of his thoughts and concepts. You become what you think.

In the dream somebody becomes a beggar and somebody else a king. But both belong to a dream. Nobody is a beggar or king. Once you recognize that you are neither, you are free.

We have a conception that by practice we shall become free. Such a person is postponing his freedom. We become enlightened in this instant only and not as a result of ten years' practice. Freedom is available now.

***

When I ask myself what this whole spiritual journey is about, I say it is nothing more than getting rid of all concepts. Am I right?

Spirituality doesn't tell you to get rid of anything. What will be removed? Where will you put it? In this world there are mountains and rivers and animals. If you get rid of them, where will they go? They have to stay here. It is better to stay with everything and with love, not to reject or accept.

Be your own Self. These things are not apart from your own Self. They are within you. Change only your viewpoint. Accept these things within your own Self as your own Self. Why not accept that all of this is me? This is a fact.

Even the hopes and concepts?

Yes. If you accept these as within you, where is the trouble? There is trouble only when we accept differences between ourselves and something or someone else. Accept that everything is within you as your own Self. Emptiness. Eternity. Whatever you call it. Everything is within that, and you are one with that. Then what will you reject? Where will you send these things?

You are whole. Where will you send anything? "I am all!" is the teaching of the Upanishads. All this is myself. Spirituality doesn't tell you to let go.

But let's try a different way. If you let go of everything, then what is left? What will be left?

You can't reject anything from the Self. If you reject, there will be frontiers between you and the Self. If you say, "Let go," there will be frontiers between you and the things you have thrown out. So it is not possible in the Truth to have any limitation, any frontier. It is whole! Either you reject everything, or you accept everything as your Self. Whatever suits you, you can do. Then you keep quiet. Become empty of thoughts and accept everything.

***

How can I remove the fear?

What fear can you have? It may be fear of the destruction of everything that you are holding. Fear that you will lose all the holdings of your mind. So you are caught in between. On the one side, you can see the destruction of everything your mind has clung to, all your holdings. On the other side, eternity is calling you. You don't like to go back, and yet you hesitate to embrace eternity. This is a transit period only. A transit camp. A flight will be announced. You can't go back. The plane you arrived on is gone and you are in the transit lounge. Wait for the call, that's all.

Since you know it is a transit lounge in which you are sitting, do not become attached to anything. This is only a transit lounge. No one will be here, and no one has been here. Do not become attached here. Let go of everything so that you can travel comfortably.

All samsara is a transit lounge; nothing is permanent. Everyone is shifting. Some are coming; some are waiting for the call. You are very fortunate to know that you are in the transit lounge. Get ready. Don't be attached to anything. You have to return home.

***

The mind and body seem to be a distraction from reality, and need a special atmosphere.

He who cannot digest anywhere needs a special atmosphere. Mind needs some abode. Otherwise, there is no mind. The thought "I want to be free" brought you here. And still you are holding on to that thought. [*laughs*]

Something beyond that also is what brought me here.

This desire must dissolve now. You are abiding in that desire now, and that won't do.

If you are on the plains and there is scorching heat, you desire to go up into the mountains. Then the desire to avoid the heat leads you to want to go to the snow. You want to go to the higher altitude to be comfortable. In every step, the heat is left behind. You go on climbing, climbing. The heat is leaving you by itself. In this desire to go to the better climate, the idea "I am hot" is completely released.

Now, here you are holding on to the concept of freedom.

But this holding on also helps me to focus on the distant mountains.

It has already helped. It has brought you here already. That idea has to disappear itself. If it is not going, you are clinging. Then, clinging to this clinging, you forget what you came here for.

You can only hold one thing at a time. When the concept of bondage brings you to freedom, then give up this concept.

Very often I feel unfree and then I feel unhappy.

That's right. Just remove "un" from your language. Why do you use "un" unnecessarily? If you don't use "un," then you speak the correct language.

Then there is no trouble.

Ah. So who imposed trouble on whom?

I imposed trouble on myself.

No, no. This "un" imposed trouble. So why do you use "un" then?

Because that's the way I feel.

Okay. Give up this feeling.

How do I do that?

By not doing it.

To me, that is very hard work.

What is?

To not do that.

No, no. You asked how to do it. I said, by not doing it you have done it. Then don't do. If you don't do, what's there?

The feeling will disappear.

And what is left?

Nothing.

Ah. In nothingness, are you happy or unhappy?

I think I am happy.

Think?

I hope!

When you say, "Nothing," then no thinking and no hope is there. In happiness, there is no thinking at all. In unhappiness, there is thinking. In any kind of happiness, there is no thinking at all.

When you are happy, do you think?

No.

When you don't think, you are happy. When you are happy, you don't think.

Yes.

So what effort do you need to make to be happy? What effort do you suggest?

This is difficult for me to understand.

Understanding is not necessary to be happy. One wants a moment of peace; then one wants to stay there and extend the moment into duration.

Don't try to understand. You are in trouble because you want to understand. Give up understanding this freedom. When you want to understand, this is bondage. Objects can be understood. When there is neither subject nor object, how can you understand?

Not possible.

No need to understand.

Master, why are there so many books and scriptures on understanding?

Even books on Ramana, just to understand.

These are nets to catch the fish who are now going to search for enlightenment. Few fish are going for enlightenment, so there is a very big net to catch these few fish in the vast waters of the ocean of bondage. Scriptures are another net to catch the fish who have avoided other nets. Now they are caught in the scripture net, which has a very fine mesh.

Another net of bondage?

The last net is scriptures; God is the last hurdle. When you renounce everything, then you are free. Free of God, free of scriptures, free of samsara.

What you have studied must be forgotten. Then you can leap forward. You cannot leap forward if you cling to the understanding of the scriptures. Then you discover that you are not to try to understand. This is leaping forward beyond scriptures. No difference in holding scriptural concepts than in holding worldly knowledge.

What happens if you are in the samadhi state and you think it is freedom?

When do you think this? Before samadhi, after samadhi? Not in samadhi. So this samadhi must be constant so you do not think anything else but freedom.

So, first, where do these concepts of freedom and bondage come from? Discover this, not to gain freedom, but to undo what you have already done.

But undoing or giving up is also doing.

Emptiness is the natural position. If I try to hold, I have added something into emptiness. Now I undo what I have done before. [*takes a wad of paper that he is holding and opens his hand, letting it fall to the floor*] What I held I have given up. The concept of bondage is not your nature. Your nature is always freedom.

With my intellect, I see that very clearly, but still—

No, no. Your nature itself is freedom. You would not seek freedom if it were not your nature. You would not search.

Everybody wants to return home. Everybody wants to return to their true nature. Freedom is your nature. Anything that you have imposed on yourself to be unhappy, to be bound, is a concept. It is an imaginary concept, so give it away. Then you can't say, "I am doing something."

Suppose you have such a strong imagination that you believe you see a ghost in a room. Then someone comes to ward off the ghost. This person says the ghost is removed. There was neither a ghost nor a removal. This is the return to your natural state.

So, from the beginning, this has been your problem. Now how should we solve this important problem? Undoing is also a doing. Better not to try. Just not to understand this thing. Undo now means you forget everything that you have read, heard, seen, felt. That is returning to freedom. Everything else has been imposed on you. All knowledge is imposed by society, parents, church.

I feel like I can't even return to freedom because it is already there.

Okay, yes. Then stop here and don't keep trying to understand it. That's all. If you try to understand it, then it starts again.

I feel that someone has hit me on the head.

This is a gentleman's hit. Don't try to understand it.

We feel it takes effort to not think and that it is natural to have desires. But it is really just the reverse, just the opposite of that. That is the illusion! That keeps us bound.

***

Questions arise and then I follow the thought to its source. From emptiness, there are no questions.

When you arrive at the Self, when was it that you were not the Self? You don't need to understand anything. When you try to understand, there arises the function of the mind. This function of the mind is the doing that takes you in the wrong direction.

MIND AND KILLING THE EGO

Papaji, a recurring difficulty for me is that my ego wants to be part of the process of becoming free. My ego want to congratulate itself by saying, "Look at me. Look at what I am doing."

Part of me says, "No, you're not coming here," but my ego, feeling like a little child, says, "Me, too! I'm coming, too!" So there isn't quite that letting go.

No need for letting go. You should make use of this very sympathetic ego. It is a nice ego, a good ego. If the ego wants to be free, it is a good symptom. First, the ego will start.

Usually, the ego doesn't want you to be free, and will tend to take you toward the objects of the senses. Mostly for enjoyment.

If the ego wants to be free, start with the ego itself. First, *I* is an ego, isn't it?

Yes.

Through this ego you are working. Everything is being worked by the ego itself in the world. Now you have to make use of this ego. Take this ego Selfward from where it arises. If she wants to be free, take this ego toward freedom. What is that? Return to its source.

Ego is a thought, isn't it? Ego is the first thought that arises in the morning. "I am Fred" is Fred-thought. So dive this ego-thought toward where it arises from.

I has taken a role of ego itself. *I*, the real *I*, has become *I* as an ego. "I am doing this; I have done that; I want that; I don't want this; I know." These thoughts arise as the ego.

Then, turn the ego back toward its source from where it arises. "My ego wants to be free," you said. So bring this ego back to its source. Then this ego-*I* will introduce you to the real source, also an *I*. When she returns to her source, this *I* will merge into the source. That is why this thought is a very blessed thought.

"I want to be free" is still ego appearing. So you must work on this ego-thought, this *I*-thought. And return back to its source. Then the ego will see her face; she will merge and ego will vanish. What will be left is the source itself. And this ego will not appear again. It will be dissolved—discharged into the ocean as a river discharges into the ocean and becomes ocean and does not return.

From there, the functions will be from the source itself! Not egoistic. Spontaneous, without involvement in the thought process. No thought process will be there—only direct spontaneous activity without thinking.

First *I* think and then *I* act. This process will be gone, and direct activity will be there according to circumstances. In this process even the memory won't be there either. You don't need memory. Memory is ego itself.

All this will be finished. Mind will be no-mind. Mind and ego, there is not much difference. Neither the mind nor the ego exist. In fact, they never existed!

These are just your own desires. Desires for the enjoyment of the samsara. Yet in reality, they don't exist.

You have never seen the face of your ego, nor the face of your mind. It is like a ghost, so as a ghost we accept it. This has been handed down from generation to generation. In reality, the ego doesn't exist, the mind doesn't exist, and samsara doesn't exist.

Yet when the ego arises, samsara arises. When the ego ceases, samsara ceases. When samsara ceases, then you will recognize your nature. You are not to earn it by any effort!

Even when you meditate it is the suggestion through the ego itself that you meditate.

The way you speak about it now, it sounds like a very loving process. Normally, I think of getting rid of the ego or killing the ego, to let it go. But now you are saying that one should let the ego see its own true nature.

Yes.

That seems like an incredibly loving thing to do for anything. Because then it isn't killing, but an enhancement. Whatever sees its own true nature would be perfect.

When you decide to kill ego, this is the ego itself. How will you kill it? Has anybody killed the ego? What is the weapon needed to kill the ego? First there must be something to be killed. First you must see the thing that is to be killed. Then, in the seeing, it is already killed.

This thought arises: "I want to kill the ego." Trace this *I* itself. When you say, "I want to kill the ego," return back to this *I* and see if there is any ego to be killed.

You have often said the ego is like a wave arising in the ocean. It seems to me that the ocean and the ego are part of the same thing. Now I see I should really sink into my ego and, from the place of the ego, recognize that I am of the ocean itself.

No, not that way. When you say the wave belongs to the ocean, who is saying the wave is different from the ocean?

Ego.

Ego is the wave. You are the source. You are ocean, yet you do not identify yourself with the ocean in that place. When you are the ocean, how do you differ from the waves? What conflict do you have with the waves?

None. But my problem is to go from the ego to the source.

This source is ocean itself. Ego plays on the surface of the ocean like a wave. The trouble is that right now you are describing yourself as an onlooker of both ocean and wave, standing somewhere on the beach. You have to identify yourself and say, "I am the ocean."

I see. I thought I was seeing myself as the wave. But if I really saw myself as the wave, then I wouldn't be separate from the ocean. So the wave can't see itself as separate from the ocean.

You have to be ocean itself. You are the ocean. When a wave arises, you be under the wave. How is the wave different from the ocean itself? Name, shape, and movement. All this is activity, but how is the ocean concerned with the wave's name, form, or movement?

Waves rise and fall and move about, and how is this the ocean's concern? You be the ocean first and then see. Where is the wave? Where is your ego?

These waves are only samsara arising from the ocean. Underneath is nirvana. Ocean is nirvana. Emptiness. In that emptiness, waves arise. And in emptiness, if waves are moving, how are they different from emptiness itself? They are all empty!

So you have to return to the source, to emptiness, to the ocean, and then see how you feel, how you are different in activities, movement, name, form.

***

What is your response to someone who says, "I have a family and children. I have too many commitments, so what possibility is there for me to awaken?"

That person must wake up from the dream that he or she has a family. One is always free and one is always alone. The mind is only dreaming. For example, when I fall asleep, I dream that I marry and have children. In the dream, I start to worry that I have no time for meditation or to go to the cave in the mountains. All these things are uttered when a person is living in a dream. It is better to wake that person up from the dream. Nothing has ever touched this person; he or she is always alone. When you see any name or any form, it is only a dream.

***

I read that Ramana Maharshi said we should constantly abide in the Self.

I would say instead, liberate the mind from any abiding.

But the mind does not abide.

Who else but the mind abides?

Yes, but the mind finishes.

Yes, this is non-abidance. If you abide somewhere, you have rejected someplace else to abide here. If you abide here, the mind will jump to abide somewhere else as well. Allow the mind to abide nowhere, and what will be the result? Mind has to abide on an object. If the object is removed, the mind cannot hang with an object. Then there will be no-mind.

Then the mind is its object.

Yes, same thing. Any object is objectified mind. And if you don't allow the mind to abide anywhere, there is no-mind. No-mind is freedom. When mind abides, samsara appears. Samsara is a construction of the mind.

THINKING AND EMPTINESS

A woman is about to be married. As was normal for someone in this condition, her head was filled with thoughts and plans and ideas for the future. She was walking from her village through the forest to the next village when a lion jumped into the middle of the road.

In that moment where is her mind? Where is her past? Where are her thoughts and plans for the future?

The future is dependent on the past. The mind is a graveyard digger! Digging up old bones from the past to chew on! So, welcome the lion in your path.

I think I experience emptiness, but it's heavy.

Emptiness is not heavy. This cannot be true emptiness. Who is thinking? Where does this *I* live that thinks? For you, *I* is also a thought. Trace it back to its source and discover from where it arises. The thought must stop. First, no object, no doing, no *I*.

This is why I do not give you a practice. If you practice meditation for one hour or two hours, for a ten-day retreat or a one-month retreat, then what about the rest of the year? It must be sixty seconds of each minute, sixty minutes of each hour, twenty-four hours a day.

That is true silence. That is true meditation. True meditation never stops! This is why there is nothing to do. No practice. Simply be who you already are!

I am giving you nothing and taking away nothing, only pointing to that which you already are. Don't leave here thinking, "I think I experienced emptiness."

First remove the activity or doing, which is thinking and experiencing, then remove the *I*. Then we can begin! Then there is room for interesting discussion. From this place report your reality.

***

I find that during satsang I fall asleep. It is pleasant but blank. Then I drift back into awareness. Should I make any effort to stay awake?

No. It is good to sleep during satsang. [*everyone laughs for several minutes*]

If you are awake in satsang and you fall asleep, and again you are awake in satsang, how can the interval be called sleep? If you have a thought "I am meditating," then a thought "I am asleep," and then a thought "I am meditating," how can you call it sleep? When you leave for sleep, where did you put the baggage of satsang?

It was still there.

Still there. And when you wake up, where did you leave this baggage of satsang? In sleep?

Still there.

Yes. This is consciousness. Consciousness does not sleep. In the waking state, it is awake. In the sleeping state, it is awake. This awareness does not change. The states may change. And you are that awareness, in waking state or sleeping state or dreaming state. There is no difference. Difference is created by the mind. And when in satsang, we do not speak our mind, only awareness. [*laughs*]

***

I have a question relating to freedom, about the use of the correct method in regard to the chakras.

Don't worry about methods. If you are sincere and honest, and have a true desire for freedom, even wrong methods will take you there. Therefore, give rise to the desire 100 percent, and the rest will take care of itself. What you are doing is not important; the end is important. You can do anything you like. The end must be that "I have to be free." You must be sincere, serious, and honest. Then don't worry about the methods. This inside Self is consciousness itself. If you do not know the correct method, it will lead you. Where you are arriving, it already knows who is coming, and it will go out to receive you in the proper way for you. You must be honest and never mind proper method.

I see that my mind is looking to own and control what is going on.

When the idea of control comes, the mind resists. Don't control the mind. Let it go anywhere it likes. Let it run anywhere in this moment, and what happens?

It relaxes.

Why?

No tension. No fighting.

So this is the opposite method, letting the mind go where it likes. All of meditation is to control the mind, and this is letting the mind go. What difference does it make?

The result is the same.

Yes. Neither will work for some; both will work for some; one or the other will work for others. It is your earnestness, your desire, not the method.

You are always in the source. How can you leave the source? This is a joke. The fish are crying, "I am thirsty." You are crying like a fish, "I am not the source. I am not myself. I am not *I am.*" What a big joke! When you come here for freedom, it is a big joke. I myself enjoy this joke. You will return to where you came from.

Well, is there anything important then, Papaji?

This is the only thing that is important. Nothing else. Only this.

Well, if it is a joke, my coming here, what is the difference between an ordinary man and an enlightened man? Is there no difference?

One difference. What is this difference?

I don't know. I am not an enlightened man.

This is the same *I am* who says, "I am not enlightened," or "I am enlightened." This *I am* is the same.

But the experience of the enlightened man?

In *I am,* there is no experience. You only have to give up the experiences that *I am* is not. "I am so and so." This is the experience. *I am,* to have an experience, has become somebody. *I am* is existence. *I am* is awareness. Finish at the *I am* and tell me what experience you will get.

And this *I am* contains all the cosmos. So there is nothing to attain or do. Just end at *I am* and see what the experience is. *I am* is eternal. Here, death can't enter. It is here in waking, deep sleep, and dreaming. Nothing to lose or gain.

To become something, to expect something, you have to do something. To remain *I am,* you don't have to do anything. Its fullness is emptiness. *I am* is the ocean, and the waves are the cosmos, the universe, all happenings. And you can enjoy. This is called Leela's sport [God's play].

***

When you give rise to a thought and don't cling to it, what happens? It returns to emptiness and so is no-thought. Only clinging creates unfulfilled desires.

If the thought arises, "I want to be free," it is not clinging, because freedom is not an object. Where does it spring from? It will merge there, and you are conscious of that. Therefore, it is called freedom. Effortless. No practice. Only see what is happening. Enough that you have attention and you are aware all the time. Even when you say, "I was not aware," you are aware that you were not aware.

The mind has a tendency to make freedom an object.

If the king is gardening, he is not called a gardener. He is still a king.

Is awareness of no-thought still a subtle thought that has to be rejected?

Also rejected.

How do we do that?

By not raising this question. If you do not give rise to this question of how to do it, what is left?

Awareness.

And how did you "do it"? [*laughs*]

***

This is just a trick of the mind.

If you call it a trick, it is no more a trick, is it? A trick is that which doesn't allow you to proceed further. This is called maya. But it is imagination only. This is no trick. You want to stop. You do not want to proceed further, so you shift the responsibility to the trick. But this is no trick. Being is no trick. You are, by nature, as you are—this is no trick. What is called a trick is that you do not want to proceed further.

***

I used to have an image of flying though space and I was scared. Now that I know there is no place to land, I still have the image, but I am not scared anymore.

So, if you have nothing to fear, why don't you identify yourself as the space itself? You are already that. It is like the wave rejecting the ocean and trying to run away from it, isn't it? "I will save myself and go somewhere else." With great speed the wave rushes away from the ocean, from this great fear of the ocean. Always she abandons the ocean, by thinking what she has to do, what she has been doing, what she was: "I will save myself."

What is all this running to the shore? It has to merge into its own substratum, into its own essence. Only the separate name and form have to go to be recognized as the ocean itself.

So when the idea of space arises, identify yourself as that ocean, as space itself. Then you can shout, "I've got it!"

***

I find questions come up to ask you, but when I follow them back to their source, they disappear.

When you know this trick, you don't need to ask anything of anyone. When you know this simple trick, you don't need to ask anything, anywhere. So stay there. That is your permanent, eternal abode. Where nothing can touch you.

When you don't stay home, you wander to the supermarket. And you make purchases and you like certain things, and so you want to stay there. You want to stay on there. That is what is happening. All these problems you are facing are only at the supermarket. At home there is no problem. No trouble. If you go home too late, you will be pushed out and the gate will be closed. It will be too late for you to return home. So do it now. Finish making your purchases and return home now.

And this home which I mention is your own Self. It is eternity. Where there are no demands and no needs and no wants, and therefore no desires. Desire is only in the mind if something is absent. You desire that thing and you run out of the house after it. Your true home is perfect, complete by itself. No need is there, you see. It is complete fullness. Full of everything. You are the lord of the place. Don't become a beggar. "I need this, I need that" is just begging about things.

***

You said, "I am not an enlightened man." Where did you get this thought? Did you not go to the past? Who is not enlightened? Past or present?

Past.

Therefore, you made an effort to go to the past—to get this concept of unenlightenment, ignorance. So don't make any effort to go to the past, and let us see what happens. Don't make any effort to go to the past or to conceive of a future.

Who are you when there is no past or future? In that split moment you are enlightened. Now where will you go if you split this instant?

Try to become ignorant! Out of this instant of light, go into darkness.

I can't.

Not possible? Good. Stay as you are. No effort is needed. You have to go somewhere to become something else. When you know it is stupid to become something, this is enlightenment. For this you do not need any effort at all.

***

Why do you use the word "emptiness" so much? You seem to really like the word "emptiness."

Everybody has some fascination about certain words. When I use this word, I speak from my experience, not for any other reason. This is my experience. And to represent that experience I don't find any appropriate word. It is an indescribable experience, where there is no trace of anything. Nothing. When I use the word "emptiness," it is the best word I can use for my experience. Nothing ever existed. You can call it empty. There is no other word available to my knowledge.

In 1919, after the First World War, I was a small boy going to school. We had a one-month vacation for the British victory. We were all given little badges and we were very happy.

My mother went to visit her sister in Lahore. I accompanied her. We were living a hundred miles toward the frontier. One evening we all went out together and we had mango shakes. Mango shakes were a common drink in the Punjab. We were sitting around a table, and they were passing the mango shakes around the table. When my turn came, I was in a situation I could not describe at that time. I had never heard of samadhi. But when they passed my glass, I did not reach up to take it or say anything.

My mother grew very afraid for me. They carried me to a nearby mosque. Even though we were Hindus, we lived within a Muslim majority, and if you were sick, you went to the mosque for help. Animal or man could be brought to the priest of the mosque, and he would say some mantras.

So they carried me to the mosque, where it was pronounced that I must be haunted by a ghost. This was reasonable to them because beyond this, they did not know.

They brought me home, and for the whole night I sat in stillness. The next morning I could again speak.

My mother asked me, "Why were you silent?" I said I did not know. Then she asked if I saw Krishna. I said, "No, nobody was there."

She wanted to know why I had been sometimes laughing and sometimes crying. What did I see? I told her I didn't see anything. That was the first time I experienced what we are speaking about. During that time I did not see anything; I was very happy. But to express that happiness, as I have been doing now for seventy years, whenever I sit, I go back to that space that is beyond time. To express that moment I use the word "emptiness," but there was neither nothingness nor somethingness. Inside I was very conscious, but I could not describe that consciousness by any name. Therefore, I use the name "emptiness."

So you could say "empty of name and form"?

Even empty of emptiness itself, let alone name and form. This word I borrowed from somewhere. I can't describe, I have no language to describe, but to speak to you, I must use some word that you understand, and that is "emptiness."

There is no time concept. No light. No darkness. Only consciousness is there. And this consciousness cannot be grasped by any imagination. Vast emptiness.

What we speak about, anybody can reasonably understand. And if it is understood, it becomes a trap. Understanding and not understanding are all in the scheme of ignorance, just a realm of the mind. This is not learning. This is your birthright. You cannot study to be what you are. You do not need to understand in order to breathe.

***

Your talks remind me of the saying "When a pickpocket meets the Buddha, he only sees his pockets."

Well, I will tell you of a master pickpocket. This master pickpocket was in Lahore, which was a major diamond center. One day he saw a man buy the perfect diamond. This diamond was the one he had been waiting for all these years. This was the one diamond he had to have.

So the pickpocket followed the man who had bought the diamond. When the man bought a ticket on the train to Madras, the pickpocket also purchased a ticket to Madras, and ended up in the same compartment. When the man went to the toilet, the pickpocket searched everywhere. When the man went to sleep, the pickpocket continued to search for the diamond, without luck.

Finally the train reached Madras, and the diamond merchant was on the platform. At this moment the pickpocket approached him.

"Excuse me, sir," he said. "I am a master pickpocket. I have tried everything without success. You have arrived now at your destination. I will not bother you. But I must know where you hid the diamond."

The man said, "I saw you watch me buy the diamond. When you showed up on the train, I knew you were after the diamond. I thought you must be very clever, and I wondered where I could hide this diamond that you would never search. So I hid it in your own pocket."

This diamond that you are searching for is so close, closer than the breath. But you search the Buddha's pockets. Empty everything from the pockets of your mind. Search where there is no distance and nothing to do. It is too easy for you.

***

You can only lose something that is in your pocket. You can only lose what you have gained. When you have an empty pocket, what can you lose? Then you need not have any fear. You can't lose emptiness. Nobody can pick the empty pocket! So empty your pocket. This is called freedom. Whatever is stored in the pocket, empty it. Then there is no fear. You can walk freely.

When the policeman chases the thief, the thief runs away. The policeman then tracks the thief back to his den, back to where he started from. Like this, as a thought arises, chase it back to its den. This den is the source. It is the source of all the thieves who have been robbing you all these years.

If you enter there, they will vacate the place.

When there are no thoughts left, the den is empty, and this emptiness is your nature. You will be very happy to settle down there. When you walk and talk now, you will function from this emptiness.

If you lose this, the ego arises from somewhere, and then you become egocentric and don't recognize who you are. Just this thought, "I am some name," is quite enough to fall back again into this.

PRACTICE AND MEDITATION

I don't find that "meditation" is really a suitable translation of *dhyana.* In Pali, the Buddha's language, it was exported to China as *dana,* where it was pronounced *chan,* and in Japan it was called *zen.* People who practice, during meditation, as observer and as object of observation actually come under concentration, or *darana* in Sanskrit. It is actually *darana* from where the question of the observer and the object of observation arises.

Darana is good to bring the mind back to one object from its tendency to run about, object to object, many times in a second. So it can be good to bring it, by concentration, back to one object. This is just like holding the tail of a dog. As long as you hold it, it is straight. When you leave it, it becomes curly again. [*everyone laughs*] It is not the nature of the tail to be straight.

Dhyana means there is no object or subject in the mind. All the rest is concentration of some sort. Concentration has to be practiced. In the practice, the mind will never be destroyed. It may be calm for some time, as long as you are practicing, but it will not destroy itself. It will not be destroyed.

So the question is whether to keep the mind calm by practice, or destroy it forever. The latter is absolutely necessary for freedom. When there is no mind, there is freedom! Concentration is practiced the world over, but I don't find any results from it. Concentrating on an object, like the breath or body, is done with some effort. Effort is needed between the observer and the object of observation. When there is effortlessness, when the mind does not function and returns to a natural state of calm, peace, this is freedom.

So, how to do it? There are different ways. Actually, to have freedom doesn't require any effort or method. You don't tread down the beaten track. You have to find your true nature, who you are.

Before trying to know anything else, or to follow any method—even those prescribed to you by the ancient saints—leave aside everything. Sit quietly and do not move your mind or intellect. Then observe the observer. This is your true nature, from where everything else comes. It is your own nature, don't forget.

If you make any effort or use any method of trying to achieve something at some distant future, this will bring you into time. And time is mind. So this will be the play of mind only. But your original nature is empty.

If you follow any thought that arises in your mind, you will find it arises from emptiness, from its source. And when you are aware, when you see "I am that source itself," then there is no need to practice anything. No need to go anywhere. And you will see that you have always been that. This is called freedom, and you are not to achieve or attain it in some distant future. It is already there. Any questions?

If one is aware that that is one's nature, when a concept of time or fear arises, it's like a stumbling block.

This is a fear of facing emptiness, because you are living in so many concepts and things. When you meet the emptiness face to face, you lose everything: all the concepts of past, present, and future which you considered real: "This is my life." Are you holding on? This is your supposed strength. This is a feeling that you are living along with your concepts. When they leave you, you have fear. Fear of dying in the ocean of nectar. Fear of death in the nectar. What is the meaning of nectar? Eternity. Deathlessness.

We cling to something for safety, and we find we are holding on to the body, the mind, the senses, for safety. We don't realize that by getting rid of these things, we have true peace. When we go from waking state to sleep, we lose everything that we held in the waking state. Relationships and possessions are lost to us in sleep. We have to let them go. We have no fear as we drop into sleep. We enjoy it; we welcome it. But we are afraid of this waking drop into emptiness because we haven't had the experience.

***

Papaji, you said that mind and objects are the same, that the objects cannot be there without the mind. Then it seems like a meditation practice, like Vipassana, that sets up that looking at objects just reinforces mind.

By the mind, yes.

It is just more mind!

Like holding on to the tail of the dog.

So what can be the value?

This has a value. To allow you to raise this question is enough value for it. Unless you hold the tail out straight, how will you know that it will return to crookedness? And that is the lesson from all the practices that are done. All the shastras and the scriptures say this is the teaching: "Reject us!" Even the descriptions: "Reject me!" This is the benefit you have been given. Otherwise you will not give up your concepts.

If you practice you will only become fatigued. When you are fatigued, you throw away everything. At that instant you are free. To get rid of everything is freedom. Everything that you do suggests, "Get rid of me." To get rid of desires is freedom, freedom from the function of the mind.

The function of the mind is desire, so get rid of the desire. Get rid of the desire for samsara. Get rid of the desire to enjoy other worlds, like heavens. Get rid of that. Get rid of the creator of heaven and samsara. Get rid of him also. After that, get rid of this renunciation. Reject all of these; then renounce this renunciation itself. Then this is freedom.

Everything you do is only to get rid of desire. You enter an educational institution for studies. Eventually all the students reject this institution; they don't want to stay there all the time. After getting a degree, though the professors may be very good, you don't want to keep sitting there. You have entered only to reject it. Everything you do suggests, "Get rid of us." Even the body will be happy when you get rid of it. All that you are doing is returning home, which is a very safe place.

And where there is no mind, there is no form. Every thing, every time, even every breath, wants to find and have peace. Even each inhalation needs rest for a moment. Before the exhale, it takes a rest in between. Nobody wants to work. Not even the breath wants to work. The breath enters emptiness for some time before entering again into functioning.

We must touch emptiness, whatever we do. We can't do without this empty moment. We ignore this moment because it is so readily available. You are not to do anything.

It happens between thought and thought also, when the mind takes a rest. Two thoughts cannot happen at the same time. Think. Stop. Next thought.

Always you are surrounded by that which you seek outside. You are inside that thing. And outside also; it is the same thing. Only we have to pay a little attention.

***

There has been a long-standing debate in the spiritual life. One view takes the relative approach of spiritual practice, developing oneself and gradually becoming enlightened, hopefully in the near future. The other view takes the position that spiritual practices are a distraction, and thereby miss the essence, which is immediate. What are your comments on the relative approach?

By any tradition, I don't think the essence can be arrived at.

Do you mean that traditional forms serve to obscure the essence?

I don't think anyone living in the traditional way has been freed from samsara. Take the case of the Buddha. He rejected all the traditions. He tried all the traditions; he found they did not bring him the thing that he wanted. He tried, but then he said he could not arrive at the essence, at enlightenment. He sat under the tree and found the essence by himself. Abandon all traditional dharmas and you will arrive at the true dharma.

***

What is your comment on insight meditation?

The observer has to observe something, such as the breath. What you observe is through the mind. So whatever is gained through the observation is only mental. Who is the observer? The observer is not tackled, only the observed, the object of the senses.

One of the features of insight meditation is realizing that the observed is impermanent, unsatisfactory, and impersonal. There is a realization that nothing is worth clinging to. Through direct observation of objects, the person experiences real changes within, bringing peace, clarity, and contentment.

I think there is a clinging to inside through something that seems outside. Remove this wall of outside and inside. For example, nirvana is inside and samsara is outside, or form is inside and emptiness outside. If you are looking for emptiness, you are somewhere outside of it. So you construct a wall between you and something unknown. If you remove this wall, you don't need any meditation.

For insight meditation there are four objects of the mind: body, feelings, thought, and sense-world objects. As you point out, there is no inquiry into the observer who seems to stand outside of all this. Where does the person go from here?

To whom does the body belong? To whom do the feelings belong? To whom do the thoughts belong? To whom do the objects belong? The body has no capacity to be enlightened because it is nothing but earth, air, fire, water. To arrive at freedom, we reject the body. We also reject the feelings, thoughts, and objects. What happens if we reject all this? Who is capable of rejecting all these things? One is neither body, feelings, thoughts, nor objects. All this is due to Self. You can reject everything, but can you reject *I?*

What do you mean by "rejection"?

We all accept that we are in the waking state, with body, feelings, thoughts, objects. Let us move toward the sleep state. In the last second before sleep, what do you do? Do you see all these things? What do you do to reject all these things and enter into sleep?

Nothing.

Unless one abandons everything, one cannot sleep. How does one enter into sleep?

One is interested in falling asleep.

That may be, but you also have to reject all these things, even your wife who is next to you in bed. You love your wife, but still you reject her. Why do you reject all these beautiful things of life, and all this samsara?

Out of necessity.

Yes. If that is a necessity, what has happened when you go to sleep? Are you not more happy in deep sleep than in the daytime?

So the entering into sleep is the simultaneous rejection of the waking state.

We can agree on that. Then you enter this sleeping state that you do not know. What is there during the sleep? Who is awake? Are you happy or unhappy in deep sleep?

Very content.

He is very content. [*laughs*] In the supermarket we purchase many things. Is contentment going to yet another marketplace, or returning home?

Returning home.

The market is the body, feelings, thoughts, and objects. If all these things could give us real contentment, we would never like to go to sleep. There is something more precious, and that is why we prefer to sleep. So, in sleep, we do not experience all those things that we speak about. Who is awake during sleep?

Nobody that I know.

Something was awake. Because the next morning you say, "During my sleep I did not think about anything. I was very happy." So, during the sleep, who experiences this happiness?

I have no idea.

[*laughs*] Excellent. Excellent.

There is the fading away of the objects—

Objects cannot fade out.

I appreciate that. This is just a form of language, not reality. Over the edge of the vastness of sleep, *I* cannot go.

Let us start from here. This waking state is samsara. Let us end body, feelings, thoughts, objects here. This ends, but deep sleep has not yet started.

This is the pure witness, pure sakshi. Meditators get stuck at this point.

Clinging occurs here. Beyond is unknown; beyond is emptiness. What is known is rejected, but beyond is not seen. Between that beyond—let us not give it a name—and things of waking condition, what do you see in this moment?

There is identification with *I*, which has an appearance of being solid and permanent.

This *I* and everything that goes with it, comes to an end, but something beyond has not yet started. It cannot go back now. In this moment it is between the known and the unknown.

It seems that the thought is making a distinction between the known, called *I*, and the unknown. The thought that it must get rid of the known to taste the unknown, to taste emptiness. So the meditator continues practicing in the effort to end this *I*.

When this *I* is facing something else, this *I* will feel shy, like a new bride. You will be happy to be brought to this point, which is not easy to speak about with language. What is in front now is what *I* has never experienced in body, feelings, and so on. *I* is fatigued with all these things, and this *I* will simply disappear.

At this critical point, is there a humility, a trust, that its own dissolution will take place?

It will embrace something else, which has no name. It is a jump into nectar with no subject and no object.

So, do you mean all the practices, meditations, traditions, and processes of "becoming" must be left behind, so a person can come to the edge?

If you give up all practices, what will happen? If you have unloaded all the dharmas, you are absolutely naked. When you are naked you will jump into the ocean, never to return.

Seriously committed people wishing to leap into the ocean come to the edge. But then the person thinks, "If I drop my practice, my method, then I will just get lost again."

Yes, fear. That person who is not willing must be pushed.

Are you a pusher?

Some people need a push. You need a push to somewhere else when you are hesitating. But then one starts a tradition of pushing. You then need a son of God, and a religion has started. Truly speaking, you don't need a push.

Why not?

You are never at the end, and you never start from anywhere else. Going to the end, to the edge, is a concept. It is only a concept of mind to think one has started from somewhere else and is going to arrive, and that, at this point, you need a push. You have never started or ended anything, and you have never needed any push.

So we do not arrive at any critical point, or come from anywhere?

There is no samsara and no nirvana.

So any construction of mind, such as being at the edge, is a complete fiction.

That is why it is called mind. [*laughs*] There is a suggestion of mind: "I want to be free from samsara." Then the practice starts, the method starts, and the dharmas start. To proceed toward nirvana from samsara is also a concept. Nirvana is a concept, another trap like samsara. But when we call it a trap, this is also a trap. We then want to get out of this trap. We know by a special spontaneous knowledge.

Then you do not need any push. You do not jump anywhere, for there is nowhere to go and nowhere to come from.

Breathtaking! Can we turn to the relative?

Yes, for there is nothing to be rejected and nothing to be accepted. You are free to accept everything and reject everything.

***

I am a meditation teacher, but I am worried because I have not been sitting now for many months.

And what have you lost as you have not [been sitting]?

Nothing.

Sitting, standing, running—it doesn't make any difference. This has nothing to do with meditation. People who are crippled sit all the time. They are not meditating. And someone who is "meditating" whose mind is running toward sense objects is not meditating.

The fishing cranes are silent and concentrated and standing on one leg—what sadhana [religious practice]!—but they are finding fish! So it depends on the mind, and the mind will trouble you even while sitting, standing, sleeping. It will trouble you. You will worry that a cobra might be coming, that a tiger is coming. It will give you fear. Mind is trouble. Day and night, it is never at rest. Even at night it is mostly dreaming. Very few minutes of real rest.

Even samadhi of yoga or practice is only another state. One day a yogi went to the king. He told the king that he could go into samadhi for forty days. For forty days he would not eat, speak, or even breathe. The king said, "If you can do this, I will give you a horse." This was what the yogi wanted, so he went into samadhi.

After forty days he did not come out. Years went by and the yogi stayed in deep samadhi. The king eventually died; the horse died. Still the yogi stayed in samadhi. The king's son was now on the throne, years later, and the yogi opened his eyes. He looked around and said, "I want my horse." This is only mind.

***

Once an eighty-year-old swami came to visit me when I was sixty [about twenty years before]. He said, "I am a yogi. I have lived forty days underground in samadhi. I only have two days, so please don't speak about yoga. I have studied all the scriptures and the Gita, so please don't discourse on these things."

I told him, "Yes, of course, I will speak about something you have not mentioned. But how about those things you are still carrying, which you have brought with you here into my room? Will you please go out of my room and leave all these things outside? And then come to me and I will speak to you, not touching this garbage which you are carrying all these years."

He didn't understand.

I said, "I'll help you, Swamiji. You bring all this garbage which you have spoken of, and I will help you to carry it and leave it outside. Then you return empty to me and I will speak about something else."

I sent him out. He stood at the door for about five minutes. Then he came in and was about to touch my feet. I stopped him halfway.

"No, Swamiji," I said. "That is not possible on three counts. First, I am a householder and you are a monk. Therefore, I have to touch your feet. Second, you are learned and I don't know how to read Sanskrit. And third, you are twenty years older than I."

He said, "This teaching no one has taught me. There were none to teach this. I am very happy. You have enlightened me now. Tomorrow I am not going on any more pilgrimages. I am finished with all that. I have about 150 students. They can go. But tomorrow, what time can I come to see you?"

I laughed. "You still want to come?"

A few days later one of his students asked me, "What did you do to the swami? He has rejected everything!"

Nobody teaches this emptiness. Everyone wants to run an ashram or commune. When you speak of emptiness, there is no more to learn. Emptiness is emptiness. San Francisco or Delhi. Wherever you go, the emptiness surrounds you. Silence will follow you wherever you are.

***

Whatever practice you are doing, continue until it leaves you. Or, if you choose to stop it, do so with respect. It got you this far and must be treated with respect.

Once a boy came to me when I was staying in Rishikesh, on the banks of the Ganga. After a day with me, he took me back to his hotel room. He showed me that he had thrown away all his books. He said that for fourteen years he had been practicing from these lessons and books, and in one day with me, he realized how worthless they were told the boy to take the books and respectfully wrap them up and offer them to the Ganga. We went together, and he threw his books into the Ganga, with thanks that they had brought him this far.

***

[Poonjaji held satsang at the zoo today. He explained that it is important to be able to take darshan anywhere.

It is important that the recognition of silence be maintained while walking, talking, eating, and mixing in crowds.]

This silence cannot be affected by daily life. Life must continue in an ordinary way.

***

What is the meaning of *dharma*?

Dharma means "the way." It has to do with concepts. The root is "that which you hold." Ways are different, different dharmas, different concepts. The highest dharma is to reject all dharmas. If you reject all concepts, all your ways, this is the dharma that will force you back to source. Otherwise, ways will take you from source to outside. When you reject all dharmas, this dharma will lead you home. Therefore, the best is the Supreme Dharma: to reject all dharma!

***

What about vasanas, latent tendencies or inherent tendencies?

These are the dormant habits inherited of the mind which are buried in memory. Accordingly, in certain circumstances, they arise to grab the object. They return to memory, where they are again embedded, and then appear again at proper circumstances.

After enlightenment, their power is destroyed because the identification is destroyed; the "doership" is not there. The viewpoint has changed. Interest is not there.

The viewpoint will be very stable, and response to circumstances will be natural. Ignorant people carry the past and worry about the future. The jnani [an enlightened one who knows through direct experience] acts according to circumstances, with no footprint in the memory.

WHAT TO DO

All doing has a goal. It starts in the past with a concept and projects into a fantasy of the future. Doing can never take you anywhere you don't already know or can't conceive of. Trace the idea that starts the doing back to its root. There you will find the end of the journey that is never begun. Doing can never get you to that which you already are. Doing is moving away from that, not toward it.

Are there still desires after enlightenment?

Before enlightenment the desire must be for enlightenment. This is not a true desire but the attraction of the Self. In order for this desire to arise, other desires must die. Ordinary desires must make way to create the space for the true desire of enlightenment.

After enlightenment, however, the Self-realized is beyond form, beyond the senses, and therefore not touched by the ordinary desires. After enlightenment the momentum of your desires may continue, but they do not touch the Self.

Once Krishna was down by the river on a holy day. The milkmaids all had offerings and wanted to cross the river to a temple on the other side. There was no boat and no bridge.

Krishna said, "Tell the river, 'If Krishna has never kissed a girl, then the river should part and make a path.'"

The women couldn't believe what Krishna was saying. It was said that he had 16,000 lovers. The river would never part! Krishna had kissed each of the women, so they doubted his words. But when they said to the river, "If Krishna has never kissed a woman, part for us," the river parted and created a dry path.

This is because the Self [Krishna represents the true Self] is immaculate and out of time. It has never kissed or been kissed.

***

I just came from seeing the Dalai Lama. He spoke of the problems of the world and the need for everyone to do right action. What is right action?

For an enlightened being there is no consideration of past or future. No consideration is given to the fruits of action. Rather, action is taken in each moment from emptiness. The fruits will take care of themselves.

The Dalai Lama was speaking to the common man who needs morality to guide his actions. Enlightened beings recognize that morality itself is empty, as is everything else. Therefore, right action, right speech, and the Buddha's eightfold path may come as a consequence of emptiness, but they will never lead to emptiness. Therefore, a seeker of truth looks for emptiness only, and everything else follows.

Then what practice do you recommend?

No practice. Let me give you an example. One day a dhobi [washerman] was down by the river when a lion appeared to drink. A hunter in the bush shot the lion. He only wanted the skin. While skinning the lion, he pulled out a baby lion and left it on the bank.

The dhobi took the baby and cared for it. The baby followed the dhobi everywhere. When it grew big enough, the dhobi put his washing on the young lion's back, along with the donkeys. So the lion grew up carrying washing on its back and being treated like one of the donkeys.

One day a lion was hunting and came upon the donkeys grazing and eating grass. He couldn't believe his eyes. Along with the donkeys was a lion eating grass.

"How could this be?" thought the lion. "Donkey is natural, good food, and there is a lion eating grass!" So the lion jumped out of the bush and started toward the herd. All the donkeys started running. The tame lion ran also. He was afraid, just like the donkeys. The hunter lion chased and caught the tame lion. He jumped on him and knocked him to the grass.

The tame lion was very afraid. "Please, sir, please don't eat me," he said. "Let me go and join the others."

"But you are a lion," the one on top replied.

"No, sir, I am a donkey."

So the hunter lion took his charge back to the river.

"Look at your reflection," he said. "We are the same."

The lion looked into the water and saw two lions looking back.

"Now roar," said the lion.

And the other lion roared!

It's as simple as that. Don't practice being a lion. Roar!

But, sir, how long does it take to realize? How long does the teaching take?

No time! How long does it take to roar? Open your mouth and it's finished.

***

I find myself doing less and less. The first week I was here I was so filled with the joy and love of your presence. Then that became a doing, a trying to recapture. Now I notice that if I am doing something, like watching my breath or sitting straighter, I notice it, and the doing stops, leaving me here in the present.

Both ideas, your doing something and not doing anything—both are impediments. Get rid of these impediments! It is not difficult. It is your nature.

If you don't do anything and give up the idea of doing anything, where do you return?

Right here.

So stay right here in this present instant. What doing or not doing is involved?

Yes. Or no. Both doing and non-doing or neither doing or not doing is involved. [*Poonjaji laughs*] It is like a child's puzzle. Each way I turn is a trap.

Whose trap is it? Who set this trap? "I want to do something" is a trap. "I want to do nothing" is another trap. This is your imagination only. Can you show me this trap?

Well, I think it is the idea of the doer who gets trapped.

Yes. So the doer is trapped inside. Finished! You are free then.

When the idea of freedom arises in most people, instantly the thought arises, "What should I do to be free?" Then they watch their diet, their behaviors, their practice—all these traps. They run to some diet or some method or some practice.

Yet, if the desire for freedom arises, take a few seconds before you start to travel. Discover where you are going. If you are going from here now, then where are you going to?

Let me tell you a story. A team of mountain climbers was scaling Mount Everest, and they camped below the summit. Another team was returning from the top and saw them camped there. "Why are you camped?" they wanted to know.

"We are waiting for our map," they replied. "We forgot our map at the base camp, and we have sent a Sherpa back to retrieve it. So we are waiting."

"But from here you do not need a map!" the returning team replied. "There are no avalanches, no problems. From here, go straight to the top! No map is necessary."

So drop all your maps and baggage. Go directly to the summit from here.

***

You say not to do anything, but some actions seem more in harmony with the Self and some seem to come from the mind. So isn't it important to do the right thing?

Spontaneous activity does not need to be manipulated by intellect, mind, or senses. Spontaneous activity will be conducted by a higher power, and it is not your concern! If you are concerned, there is doership, and then karma and the world reappear. To become a doer—"I am doing"—you become responsible. But when you return to discover where this doership arises from, it will leave you. Then some unforeseen, indescribable activity will take charge of you. Unexplainable knowledge will take charge of you. Supreme activity, unheard of, will take charge of you. That is spontaneous activity within itself, and you are not in charge.

***

Accept what comes. Reject what goes. True renunciation is neither acceptance nor rejection.

There was once a sadhu who went to market. While he was gone his hut caught fire. His neighbors saved a few of his possessions from inside his hut and were getting buckets of water from the river and pouring them on the burning hut.

When the sadhu returned and saw them throwing water on the fire, he picked up his possessions that had been saved and threw them on the fire. His neighbors looked at him in disbelief.

Then it started to rain. The rain began to put the fire out, so the neighbors stopped the bucket brigade. At this point, the sadhu started carrying water from the river in buckets and pouring it on the hut.

Well, the neighbors couldn't believe their eyes. They asked him what he was doing. He replied, "When the fire comes, I welcome and assist it. When the rain comes, I welcome and assist it."

So when a thought arises out of emptiness, do I reject the thought or the concept that it is holding?

If you are aware that the thought arises from emptiness, then this thought must be empty.

It feels like a wave arising in the ocean.

If it is the ocean, the ocean doesn't mind the waves. If there is ocean, there must be waves. These waves are samsara. Ocean is nirvana. All this is dancing.

No difference. Nothing to reject. How can you reject samsara? Where will you go? This is nirvana itself. Don't hold a dual concept that you have to reject it and go somewhere else, become a monk, change the color of your clothes, to get nirvana.

Instead, remove all colors that you have dyed the mind. Remove the mind from the clothes, and that is all you have to do. Mind has to become a monk. Don't bother with the body and its clothes.

Mind is thoughts. Mind is ego. Same thing. Wherever there is name and form, this is ego.

***

Self will not complain that my mind goes to San Francisco, because San Francisco is situated within the Self itself. All thought processes are situated in and within the Self.

All your activities, all that you do—thinking, not thinking—all arise from the Self. No problem. The problem is when the ego takes the burden "I will do" and "I have done that." If you say, "My Self has done—I have done that as the Self," there is no problem, and you will be 200 percent more efficient in your activity, even your day-to-day routine of life.

One can see the thoughts arising in the Self. California, San Francisco—these thoughts arise within the Self.

Yes, within the Self. It is not disturbing then, is it? When the waves arise in the ocean, is it a disturbance to the ocean?

So I should only think—

No. One should not think at all.

So these thoughts are the waves in the ocean, and we must remain in the ocean.

No, no! You are that! Why must you remain? You are that itself!

Yes. I have to establish myself in this.

No! No establishment either. You have to establish when you are something else. You are the Self. Now you are Doctor Boyle. Do you have to establish that you are Doctor Boyle?

Okay. I'm the Self.

I am is the Self.

I understand that *I am* the Self. And that thoughts arising in me, the Self, are like waves in the sea. Nothing more or different. Thoughts like waves merge in the ocean. They come and they merge. All these thoughts will come and merge in me.

And the ocean will have no complaint. The ocean never says, "Why are they leaving me?"

I am quiet. I am always quiet.

Yes, very good. Trouble is only for the wave that will consider, "I am something different. I am not the ocean. My name is different; my form is different; my movements are different."

So the waves, out of their ego, think they are different?

This name and form itself is an ego. Wherever there is name and form, this is ego. And some falsehood. Some fraud. Wherever there is name and form, there is some fraud.

***

What happens when we are responsible for others?

Responsibility will be executed by itself. This will be wiser because it is from the Supreme Power. Then everybody will be happier. But you do not trust this Supreme Power; instead, you trust the ego.

What was the total time that you spent in Sri Ramanashram?

No time! When you are in love with anybody, can you spend time in that atmosphere? This is the deepest bliss and you are never out of it. Time cannot enter there. Neither the mind nor the senses. Timeless instant. Then you will know that there is no time at all. Time is only ignorance. Millions and billions of years is an instant.

When you say there is no time and there never was, do you mean there is no separation from *I am?*

I am is *I am.* No time is your natural state. When you step out of this, you are instantly devoured by past, present, and future. This leads to all troubles, the many worlds, and it is all a trick of the mind. It is the mind that makes time.

When I am with the place where thoughts arise, there doesn't seem to be a particular place in the body where thoughts reside. Is this true?

No place either inside or outside the body. When you think, "I am the body," then in the body, it appears to reside.

I am still confused. Where do things arise when it is neither within nor without?

Investigate *I.I* will go. Where do you automatically place this *I?*

In the body. Is this the conditioning of the past?

If you say, "I will do it," but there is no attachment to the body, then where do you cling? There is no outside, no inside. You consider yourself the body, and therefore, emptiness or consciousness appears to be confined to the body.

In "Rip Van Winkle," a folk tale, the mind did not perceive time, but the body still aged.

All bodies age because the body is not the consciousness. The body is elements cooperating. When a man dies, the elements return. Even then you lose nothing. The elements are not destroyed; they simply return back to earth, as the breath returns to air. So there should be no grieving over loss of body. Only the fear of death is lost.

Is learning to see past lives helpful? People ask me to help them with this.

Why give them more trouble? One life is enough trouble. To help people you don't give them millions of other bodies. You don't possess the body; all this is mind only. All time is mind. Incarnations are from the body, not from awareness.

The ultimate truth is that nothing has happened and nothing will ever happen! If you believe it or don't believe it, the truth is not affected. If you know it from experience, it will help you to be happy.

As long as there is change, there must be something changeless to watch the changes. Without the screen, there can't be pictures moving on it. The screen is changeless; the movie is ever-changing. Wherever there is change, there must be a substratum of changelessness. That is your own nature. On this, body, mind, and all phenomena are projected.

***

So even if you are realized, the body must finish its course.

It has to finish its course, yes. That is one way of thinking. Otherwise, there is no course to finish. When the mind is activated, then you call it a course.

How does the manifested world exist for the enlightened being? Laws of nature and harmony, like the seasons, seem to exist in the waking, but not in the dream, state. I am confused about the difference between the waking and dream states. One seems more ordered than the other.

Looking for consistency is still looking to the mind. You have fixed the difference between the waking and the dream state. But do not speak of one state while in another state.

If, in the dream state, you are hungry, how will food in the waking state help you? Do you want food cooked in the dream or the waking state? In a dream state, if you see a friend, aren't you happy? And when a snake bites you in a dream, don't you suffer? Go to a dream doctor.

First realize, and then say, which is order and which is disorder. It is most orderly to step into freedom.

***

The longer I stay here, the more confused I get. I have the feeling that I don't understand anything anymore. I feel agitated inside. Everything is turning. I don't know what to do with that.

If you do not know what to do, then let it stay as it is.

I think something should happen.

Don't expect anything. Then it will happen. Don't have any expectations. Have you come here for expectations or to give up all expectations?

That's a good question.

I expect a good answer, too!

I think I have come here for expectations.

So are those expectations gone, or are you still carrying them on your head?

I'm confused about that. I don't know.

If you don't know, then it's all right. If you don't know, then don't think of any expectations. If there are no expectations, then you are free. If you expect, then you are in bondage. Choose whatever you want. Expectations are never fulfilled.

But I see all these people having wonderful experiences here, and I think I should also.

They have lost their expectations; therefore, they have experiences. If you don't expect anything, then what is left?

Nothing.

Nothing. Then you will be happy. Giving up expectations is your nature. Not having expectations is your nature. Not expecting anything. No expectations is sahaj samadhi.

THE VEHICLE TO LIBERATION

When people go on retreat to meditation practices, it seems like something happens for people. There is a softening and calming.

Changes will happen.

Once I went to my master because abruptly all my practices left me. I was very awake.

In 1945, I was working in Madras and doing my daily practices, which started at 2:30a.m. and went until 9:30a.m. Then I went to the office. One day the practices all left me abruptly. I simply did not wake up to attend to them.

In my neighborhood was a Ramakrishna mission, and the swami called it "the dark night of the soul." He said, "You come to me and listen to my discourse every evening at six o'clock." Someone of the Vishnu sect, a swami, said, "You have to continue. Come to attend our kirta [devotional service]. Our guru says, 'Even if the vessel is clean, you have to wash it for the next day.'"

I told him, "But if my cup is gold, I need not wash. Maybe your cup is brass."

So everyone was telling me to continue practicing, you see. But I wasn't satisfied. Because my experience was that the practices left by themselves. I loved them. I was puzzled because I could not do them. I could not sit.

So I went to my master to solve this problem. I went on my Saturday holiday. I said, "I have been practicing for eighteen years, always meditating. I woke up and didn't want to sit. I am confused about what to do."

Then he asked me, "How did you come from Madras to Tiruvannamalai?"

I answered, "By train."

"And from the railway station to the ashram?"

"By horse cart."

"Where are these?"

I said I had left them at their stations. He said, "The means brought you to a place and you rejected the means. They left you. Means will bring you, introduce you, and turn back. You can't keep sitting on the train when the ride is over. The work of the practice has taken you to your destination; now get out at the station. The work of the practice is over now and you have to face yourself—a very pleasing situation."

You will be happy to give up the means. We are so attached to the means and in love with the means and enjoyments that we forget the purpose. To go somewhere you need the means. What means are needed when you are not to move? When you are at home you do not need any mode of transportation.

A real teacher will not give you anything to do. No method. Nor can he give you freedom! He simply removes the concept of bondage. You can do it yourself. If you can't, go to a good teacher. That is the teaching of a true teacher.

***

There once was a king who had no issue and wanted to adopt a son. He said to his minister, "Open the gate and let everyone come to see me between eight and six. When a man comes, arrange a bath and perfumes and then dress, then lunch and music and dancing. So when a man comes to see me, he should be refreshed and relaxed and well-dressed, so that I may adopt him as a son."

The gates were opened and everyone in the town came. People were taking baths, and those fond of swimming were in the swimming pools. Others started picking up perfumes and bundling up the bottles to be carried home.

Then lunch started, and everyone started bundling up boxes of food to take home. Next came the music and dancing.

Then it was six o'clock and the king said, "What happened? Nobody came to see me."

The minister replied, "We don't understand, Your Majesty. We opened the gates and everything was given. In the end, everyone left carrying bundles on their head to take back home." The purpose was forgotten along the way.

What is the purpose of human life? To return home. To meet the king. To get the throne. We forgot. And then at six o'clock, the police come and throw you out. Time is over. If you go straight away to the king, all these things will be added on to you. They belong to you. Why don't you go and meet the king first? You don't have to bundle up all these things. These things belong to you. We forget the purpose of human life. You have to return and see the king. You start enjoying this thing and that thing and then the time will be over, the gates will be closed. So, it is time. And this time is this moment. So dress well, have a bath. Swim, wash, perfume yourself, eat well, and go to meet the king.

***

You say that although means get you somewhere, they have to be rejected.

Yes. This is because when you really arrive, you see that the means are totally useless, and your arrival was not the result of any means. When I saw the position after these means were rejected, I found these means had nothing to do with this situation. Once you have touched the philosopher's stone you cannot turn back to iron or brass, because you are pure gold. If means were involved, you could reverse it.

We speak of means because otherwise no one understands. But once you experience, you will see that means are of no use. Nothing touches it. Means mean mind. The mind is not responsible for leading you to that which is beyond the mind. Mind will lead, of course. These means will lead you to something related to mind. But going beyond the mind has nothing to do with means. And means belong to the past. When you speak of means, it will take you to the past. To be as you are now at this very instant, what means are needed?

CHOOSING SAMSARA OR NIRVANA

You are afraid to cross the road to the other shore of freedom because you see a snake coiled in the middle of the road waiting for you. Each day you come back and see the snake and are afraid to continue. One day someone comes from the other side and says, "It is only a rope. There is no snake, only a rope." This authority tells you the truth, and you realize it. What doing is involved here? What did you do to the snake? Where did the snake go? "I am bound" is the same snake. The snake never existed. You must remove the impediments of fear and doubt. See the rope as it is.

Whenever there is duality, it is a dream state. Whenever you see multiplicity, you are in a dream state. Creator, creation, heaven, hell, or anything in between is a dream state. When you wake up, nothing ever existed. No gods, no creation, and nothing created. No world and nothing in it. That is total emptiness.

Then the first thought comes: "I am Katherine." In deep sleep, nothing existed. No friends, no enemies. Nothing. In the morning when you wake up, instantly the first thought: "I am Katherine." Instantly, there begins the whole thing.

Time and karma appear with the first thought. So take this first thought, "I am so-and-so," and find out where it comes from. When you search, this thought will leave you, and you will recognize who you are.

On this thought, "I am so-and-so," all other thoughts depend. The entire cosmos arises in relation to this thought. So take hold of this *I*-thought, the first thought. This *I* will vanish and leave you alone. This ego-*I* will help you to return back. Then you will know that nothing ever existed.

***

So you are saying we sometimes choose to see the illusion?

Yes. This is also illusion. [*laughs*]

When you become the seer, you see the illusion and then it does not exist. To see something you must look at it. To do this you must first separate yourself. This is the illusion.

So there really is only one desire?

One desire is no desire. How can you call it one without the concept of two? You cannot call it one unless there is something else. If you are seated all alone in a room and someone comes to see you, you may say, "Come in, nobody's here." Nobody's here, you say! One desire is no desire. It needs the support of the other desires to be one. When the others go, one is not there either. It is only from duality that we speak of oneness.

***

Why do I choose to believe the illusion?

You made the choice.

But why?

You made it. You can also reject it. You are satisfied with this illusion. You have relationship with this illusion. Therefore, you believe it. If you made another choice, "I don't want illusion," then there is no illusion. It is your creation, your own imagination. The illusion does not exist.

And what do you mean by illusion, first of all? That which does not exist is called illusion. A mirage in the desert. It is your choice if you swim in it and proceed further. Your choice. And it will trouble you. If you proceed further toward the mirage in the desert and jump in to swim in it, whose choice is it?

You may never go swim in that river again. It doesn't exist. Only you choose it. And this wrong choice is called samsara.

To get out of this you must give rise to another choice. "I want to be free," also your choice. "I am in illusion," also your choice. So these two choices are there: whether you want nirvana or samsara. Choose one of these.

You chose samsara and now you do not see what is nirvana. Nirvana does not appear after you have chosen samsara. Once you have chosen samsara, you do not have the choice to be free of the desires of samsara.

So you do not know whether nirvana exists. You were born here; you will stay here; you will die here. And this endless cycle will continue.

Someday you have to think wisely of what is good for you. Then you have to make a choice for something you have not seen. All these people of this world are lost in that choice which you also have inherited. You see all the people who have made the wrong choice, who are all going this way, believing someone else's choice! You are also going this way, believing someone else's choice.

Why is it that some kings have made this choice for freedom? Why did they leave their palaces and wives and treasures? Buddha was a prince himself and he made this choice. What problems did he have? He had a beautiful wife and son, all the luxuries of life. Why did he make this choice: "I want to be free"? He saw the suffering in the world. He had all the comforts and luxuries of life, elephants, a kingdom. Why did he make this choice?

It is the only choice.

If it is the only choice, why have so few chosen it? Why do we still follow the Buddha's choice 2,500 years later? Some lucky people will inherit this other choice. They will have had different forefathers. They will have inherited their forefathers' choice. So you have to shift your community, your involvements.

Which is the beneficial choice for you? You have been trying this one choice for millions of years, and you can continue to seek enjoyments there. There is no end to this. One day you make a choice of no more of these enjoyments that lead only to suffering.

I don't know how to go back.

Go back where?

Back into that freedom.

If you do not know, then you know it very well. Why did you come here and not go elsewhere?

There is nowhere else to go.

If there is nowhere else to go, then this is a choice you have made. Yet you are still resisting, not accepting, your own choice. You must honor the choice. You are very lucky to have this choice. You must honor it.

I do. But something is holding me back.

Only the desire must be there.

But what stops me?

You see some friends playing on the beach, and you want to join them to play in the sand.

I do not know the way.

There is no way. To be lost you must be somewhere else, not here. You must honor this choice. Once you glimpse the face of the true diamond, you must honor it by giving it its true value. You must give 100 percent value to it or lose it forever. Why forever? Because next time you will remember that you had this experience. Give it full value and do not depend on next time. If you compare, you lose it to the past. If you lose it, you lose it forever. So give it full value, full honor.

Are honoring and loving it the same thing?

Same thing. Enlightenment takes place in a finger snap. Here and now!—rarest of all. Nearer than your breath. Why postpone it for another hundred years? If something is most near, nearer than the breath, where do you have to go, what do you have to do, to find it?

I got it!

Got it? Good! No effort is needed. Nothing to do. What is already here, very near, this is the honor. If you got it, you can never lose it. How can you lose what has no location, nearer than the breath?

***

It seems that each moment I can choose to be free. But is there another step when finally there is no choice? Are there different levels of freedom?

No. There aren't different levels of freedom, only different levels of the choices you make. Once only is enough to choose freedom. If you repeat it, it will lose its value. Hold on to the choice when it arises, and march into that choice itself. Then it will become choiceless. Identify yourself with the choice. Immediately dive into it and then that choice will be no choice. Jump into this choice and become the choice itself.

Investigate where this choice comes from. Whose choice is it? This will lead you to choicelessness. When the choice is from the other side, there is no choice. From this side it is the choice of ego, who has fooled you for ages. One call from the other side is enough. The emperors have left their thrones, families, wives, and treasures. They gave full honor to this choice.

LEELA

The waves are always washing against the shore. This is their movement and their noise. One day a little wave saw a large, old wave come rolling in from far away. The little wave asked the old wave, "Have you heard of the ocean? Is there really such a thing?"

The old wave replied with a crashing roar, "I, too, have heard talk of the ocean, but I have never seen it with my own eyes."

The waves, their movement and sound—this is called samsara. This is the illusory separateness that causes suffering. Who here can describe the ocean?

My first day in satsang, I looked out through a window. I could see birds. Those that were close passed by very quickly. Those that were far away, floating way up in the sky, took a long time to pass by my window. I realized that those birds are like my thoughts. I observed those thoughts until they didn't come anymore.

Now, out of my empty bliss, a thought is arising. I am ready for a new name. I realize that I was afraid to voice this thought. In observing this I see that all doubt and fear resides only in the mind. The bird of New Zealand is a kiwi. It can't fly because it had no predators and therefore lost its fear. [*he begins to cry*]

In the night you came to me. I knew then it was time to give you a new name. Your name is Dharma. You are the first one to carry this teaching to the land of the kiwis, as Bodhidharma took Buddhism to China.

A thought is arising about emptiness.

Good! Now identify with that thought.

The thought comes from emptiness. If it is a thought about emptiness and you identify with that thought, this is pouring emptiness into emptiness. There will be no separation. And then the thought will return again to emptiness.

Now, if this thought of emptiness arises and you check that thought, this again is duality.

***

I stop people from dropping into samadhi in satsang. All samadhi has duration. The unchanging is ever-present. Be it in traffic with full presence!

I find myself needing to withdraw from social contact.

If you want to be a saint, there is a prescribed set of behaviors to cut off worldly sensations, and being a saint is acceptable here. Some sects go so far as to avoid eye contact with women, and the Nagas do sexual organ mutilation.

However, in my experience, it is best not to change anything you are doing, as that will take care of itself. Emptiness is always alone and unchanging. It is now. Now itself is empty.

Just play your role in the Leela [the divine play] with no expectation or attachment.

***

Why do you come to me only in the waking state?

When the guru comes in what you call the waking state and wakes you up, it is only the dream state from which the guru is waking you.

Then what is the difference between the dream state and the waking state, in reference to the guru and waking up?

No difference. When you see a tiger come after you in the dream state, what happens?

I have fear and run and then wake up.

Likewise, in this so-called waking state, when you see the guru coming after you, what happens? No difference. When you wake up, you must have been sleeping. The guru tells you to wake up. If you don't wake up, you have not seen a tiger. You have seen a sheep.

There is no difference between an animal and someone who merely eats, sleeps, and has sex. Humankind, however, has the potential to want freedom from the whole process. The animal has no choice. You have the option to be free. You need not go to the slaughterhouse. You can avoid the slaughterhouse if you want to.

Otherwise, you will be taken by the butcher, the king of death.

Right now you can avoid it. Death will take the body only. You have to know right now: "I am not the body. My body is in pain. My mind is not tranquil." Already it is separate from you. Whose body? Whose mind?

Always it is your true nature, the Self, the unknown, which is responsible for the activity, but the ego claims it. When the sun is shining, you say, "I see." When the sun is gone, you say, "I can't see." Who is it who can see that you can't see? That I call Self-nature, through which seeing and not seeing is seen. You have to surrender to that supreme unknown emptiness and function from there.

***

Even though I feel so much peace and happiness being here, even being in emptiness, still the idea arises to do something. I feel it as a cloud.

No, it is not a cloud. It is a mist.

Even if thoughts come to do something, no problem. You can do 100 percent, while knowing absolutely that it is coming from the emptiness.

The sun shining, the clouds moving—all this comes from the emptiness. You will be more active, yet that acting will not disturb or trouble you, nor will it stupefy you.

There will be a role for you to play. Allow, and the activity will be there from the emptiness. Then this so-called activity will be empty.

I don't tell you to go to the monastery; instead, go on the battlefield and fight. This activity is equal to inactivity. Substratum is inactive, and you are that. Activity/inactivity has nothing to do with your status. Very spontaneous activity leaves no impression on memory. Samsara leaves footprints in memory. Your footprints will be like the bird flying. What you store in the memory is never-ending samsara.

If you know your Self, this baggage is destroyed. If you know your Self, there has been no samsara at all. Not at that time, nor before, nor after. This is only imagination and the result of one thought: "I am the body." If you remove "the body" from the sentence, what do you see?

To see samsara, you have to become the body first. Then time and multiplied millions of bodies. Just imagination. When you wake up you will see that this is an instant of time. When you get freedom you will know this very well.

***

Nature is changing. Now, some people are concerned about nature and the planet. Many minds are working on the problems of pollution and atmospheric changes. There are some spiritually minded people who even pray for the weather. What is all this?

This is also the working of nature.

No, it's the working of mind. I know that.

Yes. And where did you get this mind from?

I know. That is the mind.

Yes, it is the mind. But where did the mind get its power to work on this? Whose power did the mind get to work like this?

The Self, the source.

Yes. That source is called nature. If the mind is making some problems, it is also the nature working. Mind is also the nature.

Is the planet itself like a being?

The countless planets and solar systems hanging in space—this is all the creation of mind. Mind has tremendous power. You can do whatever you want. If you are not working toward freedom, the mind can show you that path also, if you want to make use of it. Mind is pushing you. If you say, "I want freedom," this is the association with the mind, and the push of the mind only. Mind wants to be peaceful, so why don't you have friendship with mind itself?

Friendship?

Mind is your friend and also your enemy. You can use it as you like. As you wish, so will it happen. As you wish, so will you become.

But medicine has the power to heal the body, and that is not mind.

That is mind with a capital M. It is the mind which likes to reach to the Mind. The direction of the mind is to the Mind itself, and that Mind is absolute.

Thought is within the mind itself. When it returns to the mind, it is a quiet mind, an ocean without waves. And when the waves rise from mind they become the universe.

Is Satan the mind?

The evil power of the mind is the demon. This is also a reality within the realm of mind. Mind has an evil tendency, and that tendency is manifested as a demon. In Sarnath one of the temples shows paintings of the Buddha sitting under the bodhi tree. All the temptations are shown. Armies with javelins are coming to attack him, to keep him from enlightenment. These are the stored-up tendencies of mind rising up, your own tendencies, your own creation. When there is no mind, no universe, no God, when you quiet the mind, all phenomena end.

How do you quiet the mind?

By looking at it. Look at it, and it will be quiet. Then it will be objectified. Some subject must be there to look at this object. Then you are separate from what you are looking at. Discover whose mind is agitated or whose mind is at peace.

When you say "whose mind," it's one of the best jokes I ever heard.

Yes. You are joking, and so I am joking. When you say, "My mind is agitated," you joke, so I joke.

***

I have heard you mention *Leela*. What do you mean?

What is Leela? Leela is like going to a movie. First there is the screen, and it is blank. The light is shining on the screen, and it is clear light. Then the projector starts and the movie appears on the screen. People marry and die and love and fight, and then the movie is over. The screen is again blank. The actors all the while know they are actors. No one is born; no one dies. The actor plays a king, but all the while he knows he is an actor.

After realizing emptiness, is there still preference and taste?

Yes, but it is empty. It is only the role of the king or the slave who has the taste. As soon as you identify with the role, as soon as you believe the movie is real, this is samsara.

***

Once a king was out hunting all night. He came home the next morning, and his guru was waiting up for him. The king said to the guru, "First I will take a short rest."

In a little while he woke up and said, "Guruji, I have a question. I just had a wink of sleep. During this sleep I was a beggar. One day I was going to the village to beg, and many other beggars were there. But they were all going in the other direction. I was going to town, but they were all leaving."

"One of these beggars said, 'Where are you going? Today is the birthday of the king. Come with us, and the king will give us clothes and great food and money.' I went with them and was fed and given new clothes. I decided that today I would bathe and put on the clothes the king gave me, and today I would eat like a king."

"While I was bathing, a dog ran off with my food. I chased this dog with a stick. I got the food back from the dog, and then I woke up. In this instant I was a beggar who had come to beg from the king on my own birthday! Guruji, tell me which is true. In that moment, was I a king or a beggar?"

The guru replied, "Both are dreams. In this instant we are in a sleep state as well. The entire world is sleeping. Sleeping means begging. Everybody is begging something else. Kings are begging. Everyone is begging."

Now you have to wake up, while everyone else is sleeping. Whoever stays in the Self, thinking of the Self, speaking of the Self, is in a true waking state. And when you forget it—"I am not the Self, I need something else"—this is a sleep state, and then you chase the dog for food.

DESIRE

What is the difference between my will and God's will?

You are imposing your will on the god. You say, "Let thy will be done"; you really mean, "Let my will be done." You are telling God, "Let my will be done." God has no will because he has no desire. So, really, it is "Let my desire be done." Who is it that imposes this will on God? God has no will. This is your will, your desire. God doesn't say, "Let my will be done." When it is fulfilled, it will be your own will fulfilled. God in heaven is not your attendant.

What is the will?

Desire only. Without desire, where is the will? You can actually utilize your will only once. That one time is the will to freedom: "I want freedom. I want to be free." Use your will only for this purpose. Then all will is fulfilled. Otherwise, it is no use using your will to chase this thing and that thing.

Why don't people want enlightenment?

Because the mind engages them in the enjoyment of the senses. And they fear giving up the pleasure of the senses. You can count on your fingers the number of people who truly want to be free.

Everyone is afraid: "I will lose the world, my attachments, my relationships, my dear ones." This is a foolish concept. On the contrary, when you are enlightened you will begin to have really good relationships, even with the animals, even with plant life. You will love everyone. First enlightenment, then you will be a good human being.

What pushes us to want freedom?

Good luck. A mountain of merits are accumulated; then you will want to be free. If you miss in this life, you will carry over to the next life until there is a mountain of merit.

What would you tell someone who does not have the desire for freedom? How can they accumulate merit?

Those people don't come to me. If you are looking for diamonds, do you go to a potato shop?

Aren't merits involved with time and therefore the mind?

Yes. When you cross beyond, then I will speak to you in a different language. No merits or demerits or gods or practice.

So is merit related to worthiness of the soul?

All these things are only in the scheme of ignorance. Really, there are no merits, no demerits, no bondage, no enlightenment, and no search for enlightenment. This is the ultimate truth. If you agree to this, then I will speak on this matter.

You come for freedom; in truth there is no difference between bondage and freedom. If you want to be free, this is from the viewpoint of bondage. When you are ready to reject both bondage and freedom, this is the freedom I speak about.

There is no merit, no practice, no gods, no sadhana. True meditation for freedom is pure, immaculate. No thought of freedom may enter. And this meditation is over in seconds. As long as the concept of freedom is there, you are bound. Do not have any concept, not even that you are meditating. When

I see someone meditating like this, I wake them up.

Are you saying that meditation for freedom is itself bondage?

Yes. When you run to the idea to meditate for freedom, where are you standing? In bondage or not? Do you not have an idea in the mind that you wish to be free from something? So you sit in bondage. You are meditating on bondage, not freedom!

This freedom you are looking for is the opposite of bondage. True freedom has no opposite. So start your meditation sitting on freedom itself. Have freedom in your hand, and then what are you meditating for?

Nothing.

Ah, that's it. How do you know it is nothing? It has no name, no form, no concept. Meditate on that, within that, for that. Okay? It cannot be conceived or achieved or attained. [*much laughter*] Transcend this thought of freedom. Then freedom won't be there. Knowledge won't be there. [*more laughter*]

What happens to the senses?

First you experience. First attain that state and then report. You are asking,

"After I marry, will I have a son?" Why don't you ask, "After I marry, what happens when I am fifty?" Why not ask me that? First experience. First have the wedding. Then you will know everything.

What happens to the senses when you are sleeping, to begin with? When you are sleeping, there are no senses; there is no mind, no worry, nothing. This is the sleep which is still ignorance. The mind grows tired and relaxes, and you give up everything. For four or five hours the mind temporarily relaxes and lets go.

And you have a thought to wake up tomorrow at six o'clock. With this thought, you tie a rope and then enter sleep. "Tomorrow I will do this thing and that thing." And that rope you tie around your head to wake you up tomorrow. Sleep is where you lose everything. But that sleep is filled with awareness. You are quite aware during that sleep. Now you discover.

***

I can't will myself to change. You can't will yourself not to have desires, because that is more of the ego, isn't it?

This will cannot be rejected so easily. This will, "I want to be free"—let's call it the last will, the last desire for the highest thing, which is perfection, eternity, emptiness—it cannot be rejected. It will take you somewhere and then it will vanish. This desire will burn itself out, and what will remain is your nature. So be thankful for this will. Very few lucky people will choose this freedom. Cling firmly to this desire, and it will take you to freedom and then vanish. Every desire needs the support of another desire. Otherwise, one desire is no desire. Therefore, it is freedom itself. There the means and end are the same. Intense desire for freedom alone, allowing no other desire to rise, is freedom itself.

Once you consciously know you are free, desires will rise, but they will not have a ground because these will be roasted seeds. They will not have sprouted in the memory. You will already know the end.

All desires actually end in freedom. Your desire is fulfilled and you are empty. The emptiness brings you happiness, but it is unconscious. You attribute your happiness to a possession, not the emptiness. It is the freedom from desire that gives you happiness.

All attraction is Self to Self. No body can give you happiness. It is not the body, not the meat, that gives you happiness. It is Self to Self. Attraction is Self to Self. This is the secret. Once you know it, there will be only love in the world. Hatred cannot be there.

Only an instant is required for this recognition. Once only. Just a moment. Look into and recognize your Self within this instant. You don't need a long program spread over years to recognize this freedom. You are already free. It is only recognition that isn't there, that you are postponing. You must recognize your own nature or you will not be happy.

***

Lately, the desire for freedom has grown. I feel a fire and strong desire for freedom, so strong I can barely stand it. It has intensified and burns inside so much I can hardly stand it. This desire for liberation is flaming inside. I cannot postpone it. I must have it now. I want to know immediately. Desire still burns.

When this desire itself is burnt out, then there will be freedom. You must give more intensity to this desire—much more—so that it may be consumed in its own fire, resulting in freedom.

How does it become more intensified?

When there is no support whatsoever for any other desire.

By the removal of all other desires?

Only the desire for liberation, with no association of any other desire. When there is no other desire except liberation, how can you call it a desire? If there is even one other desire, then you can call the desire for liberation a desire. Where there are no other desires left, how can you call it a desire at all?

I don't know.

You must know. Put yourself in that situation.

I still don't understand.

If there is only one desire left, without the concept of the second thing, or second desire, how can there remain one in the absence of the second? Where are the limits of this one if it is not defined in relation to something else? When there is no second, this desire will also go away, and then that will be freedom.

This desire for freedom is not going to win you anything. It will disappear, that's all. Otherwise, you would have to achieve something or attain something. Then you would lose it, and then it would not be your nature. Your nature is not to have any desire.

The desire doesn't seem to be on an object; it seems to be on the Self.

This desire arises from within the Self to attain the Self. It will return to where it arises from. It will go back. It will not take you from this place to somewhere else to be fulfilled. This desire will disappear. If you don't even give rise to this desire for freedom, what will be left?

I don't know. It has always been there.

Don't give rise to it and then see, what is the situation?

No desire then? Not even the desire for freedom?

Yes. [*pause*] Now, what is this? What is left?

First, all desires vanished, and this desire for freedom was left. When this desire for freedom also left, what remained was freedom.

When you say "freedom," is there any desire for freedom now?

No.

What happens now?

No desires.

So stay as this! What trouble is there if you stay like this? What would you call this situation: bondage or freedom?

Neither.

Yes, very good. When you say neither bondage nor freedom, in between them both now, give rise to desire. Then I will see what we will do. What desire comes? What thought comes? What object comes? What subject is left?

Nothing.

Very good! Very wise man.

***

If there is any method, it is to reject everything that can be rejected. When you have rejected everything that can be rejected, what is left is yourself. You can never reject yourself. Can you say, "I am not I"? Being cannot be rejected; all that can be rejected is becoming. What you become can be rejected. But Being, which is empty, which is nature, which is source—how can you reject the emptiness? Can it be rejected? If it is something, it can be rejected. But if it is empty of all things, empty of all ideas, how can it be rejected? Now you have to recognize, "I am this."

So when a desire arises, should we reject this desire?

No, don't reject it. Find its source. Turn back to where the desire originates; find it and you will find the source of all desire. If you have to meditate, do it this way. Investigate and discover the source of this desire. Where does your desire to meditate come from?

Dissatisfaction.

Where does this dissatisfaction come from? Go back to where it comes from. Does it come from the world?

No.

Okay, so reject outside. This dissatisfaction came from inside. Return to this inward source of dissatisfaction.

It came from my mind.

Where does the mind come from? You said "my mind." Whose mind? Find the source of mind. Satisfaction and dissatisfaction are in the mind, right?

Yes.

So find the source of the mind, which is sometimes satisfied and sometimes dissatisfied. Now trace the source of the mind. Go back to where it comes from, now.

***

It seems like the desire to be free is like the queen ant of all desires. You can spend forever going after all the little ants, or just go after the queen ant and that is the end of the ant colony.

[*laughing*] Yes, yes. Looking for the source of the mind, or "I want to be free," there is no difference. The desire for freedom is the same process of returning to the source.

When you were searching for the source of mind, which other desires trespassed?

The desire to come up with something. The desire to really know. I feel like I know the words.

Reject the words, including the word "mind" itself. What you were asked to do is to return to the source of mind.

I find quiet.

Okay. Before, you said "dissatisfaction." In this quietness, do you find dissatisfaction?

Not in the quiet itself.

So, when you return to the source of the mind, you find quietness. Who is quiet?

I am.

Then stay here and tell me if you see dissatisfaction anywhere around. "I am," you said. So question to *I* and question to *am* to find any dissatisfaction. These two are left: *I* and *am*. So let the *I* question the *am* and the *am* question the *I* to see if there is any dissatisfaction. Who is dissatisfied?

When they question each other, they are not dissatisfied.

Okay. Reject one of these now. Reject *I* or reject *am.* We are still tracing the source, you see.

I reject *am.*

Excellent. Just the *I* is left then, so question to this *I,* "Who are you?" *I* questions *I.* "Who am I?" There is no second left, so let this *I* question itself. You say, "I am Bill." Do you ask anyone else, "Am I Bill?" Who is Bill? Where am I?

Nothing.

Nothing. So even this *I* vanishes here. The word "I" disappears. When there is nothing to question, you can reject even *I,* okay? What is left now? Go beyond where the *I* arises from. Do it quickly. No thinking. You are very close. Don't miss this moment. [*long pause*]

Okay. When you say "I," what do you see? Any name? Any form?

In *I,* no.

No name, no form. That is your nature. Will you recognize it now? Will you discharge into it?

If you can't speak, it doesn't matter. I am satisfied. Only stay as such and keep quiet. Honor this situation by keeping quiet and becoming quietness itself. When you are quietness itself, then try to jump out of this quietness. Where will you go?

***

I've been feeling so much energy and bliss. You said bliss is also to be moved through.

Bliss is the last sheath to reject. In bliss there is still an activity of someone enjoying something else. Separation. Most people get stuck here. They find some happiness or bliss, and they cling fast to it and don't go beyond.

I sometimes feel so much energy when I am with you that I can't even hear what you are saying. When you said, "Go beyond bliss," I started crying and crying.

This energy is not different from the source. This energy is responsible for the sun shining, for the wind blowing, for you meditating. The problem is when you attribute this energy to something else, maybe physical, mental, intellectual, vital, or blissful. Through this energy itself, we feel happy, we breathe—this is the undercurrent. When you understand, there is nothing to do about it. Only shout a roar, "I am this energy!"

There are moments when I feel that I am this energy. Then other times the mind says I must do something.

Even then this energy is with you. "I am doing," you say, but what is the energy that lets you do? I lift a hand; what makes the hand lift? What is this undercurrent? We don't recognize it because it has no name or form. What makes the mind meditate? That is called emptiness.

You don't need any method, any practice, any concept, any book. Any way, any thing, any practice, will take you away from that. Any doing will take you away from it, not toward it.

Look for the silence. What is it? Where does it come from? How do you differ from that silence?

Anything that appears is not true. In the desert you see a river mirage and you are thirsty. The more you chase it, the further away it moves. You can never quench your thirst in that river. This is samsara. You want to quench your thirst and you move toward an object of enjoyment and you get no enjoyment. Once you know, by your experience, that it is only a mirage, that no river exists, this understanding alone is enough. You will not run after these things. You will stay where you are.

This is the rise of desire, to quench the thirst running after a mirage. And nobody is happy running after imaginary rivers in the desert. Nobody is happy. One desire leads to another desire. Who is there that says, "I am satisfied"?

So we have to turn to that which is beyond suffering and misery. All the appearances are not true. They were not there before the beginning, and they will not be there after the end. When a desire is fulfilled, for a moment, you are happy. If you watch closely, you will see it is not the object that gives you happiness. In that moment, there is no desire and your mind is empty. This emptiness gives you happiness.

There is no difference between desire and samsara. No desire, no samsara. The whole world is chasing the fulfillment of desires. When you've had some experience, after some time, you will not desire anything. That perfect state is called light wisdom. The desire for freedom itself must be abandoned. This is the last desire. Then you will cross to somewhere else. You will recognize that you are everything. Then what can you desire?

Master, by your grace, I've noticed all desires are gone. I didn't do anything. They just left.

Desires don't exist. If you touch that point of who you are, you are fullness itself. What can you desire?

Only to come back to see you.

REALIZATION

Everybody knows very well the direction that has been said and heard and known. I want to take you in the direction that has been unheard, unsmelled, unsaid, unthought. No mind has ever entered there. The mind retreats after facing the light. The shock, what you call fear, is this fear. Taking off is a fear. Once you take off you can't return to the same runway. Where are you going to land? If you know, tell me.

You have launched us into space and left us there.

[*laughs*] You can't abide. Don't cling, even to the emptiness. You can never touch any port. Because you left everything behind. What is unthought, unseen, unimaginable—this I call emptiness. Take off from the emptiness itself. Emptiness is a concept. Freedom is a concept. Enlightenment is a concept. They have brought you from other concepts, such as "I am suffering, I am bound." You have to accept concepts of freedom and emptiness. I advise you to take off from there, from freedom, from enlightenment, from any concept of whatever it is. Nobody has seen tomorrow. This instant is the time. Don't postpone this instant for the next day.

***

After we talked I felt much emotion and a very powerful longing for freedom. Then I felt that all the world wants freedom, that everyone yearns for it. It was a relief to recognize that it is not just about me, but that I am just an expression of that.

Yes, excellent. We are all returning to our source, and it is not an individual question. All the beings of this planet are only you. This thought of freedom is consolidated, belonging to everybody. If one individual frees himself, all have been freed. How do you explain this?

Supposing you sleep, and during the dream, there are many, many people who are aspiring to liberation. They are doing different exercises and practices. You are telling them what freedom is. You are speaking to everybody.

Meanwhile, someone asks you how to attain freedom.

He questions you about it, and instantly you wake up while speaking about freedom. When you wake up from this dream of others aspiring to freedom, what happens to those you left behind?

They have returned to the source.

When you woke up you did not leave anyone behind, bound. This is only the imagination that we are bound. All are free. Who is not free? When people are bound they are sleeping, and they are all projected on you. In the dream there are all those people aspiring to and working for freedom. When you wake up, where are the others?

It is a fact. Very difficult to understand, but a fact. Nobody is bound and, truly speaking, none created. None has been created. Everybody is in the source and is free. Nothing and no one is out of the source. Where can they to run to get out of the source to be free?

***

Who is journeying for freedom? The one who is already free. Just get rid of the concept "I am the body, separate from the source." You return to what you always were. This journey will take you back to your home. It will not push you to any new kind of dimension. You cannot become or get what you are not. You have to be what you already are.

When you wake up from the dream, nothing else existed! Where there is name and form, there is still dreaming. Where there is name and form, there is fraud, not reality. In the waking state there is no difference between man and man and birds and rocks, all total being.

When you aspire to freedom, the whole cosmos is with you. Keeping free of any thought is the best way to help the world when the world is crying for peace.

Papaji, will you say a few words about why, when a man receives the grace, he becomes outspoken like a lion, completely unbound, calling a spade a spade?

There remains no fear of limitation. Anything you were involved in was bound by beginning, middle, and end. When you transcend, it is boundless, beyond the frontiers of the mind. Now there is no fear. Now you can respond fearlessly. You respond spontaneously from moment to moment. There is no imagination of the future. You are living in the present, which is living free. If, however, you are related to persons or things, and you are afraid of losing something, this is bondage.

When you say that fear is about losing what has never been gained, I don't understand.

Fear is always of the past. Someone once challenged this and said, "When I leave here, if I see a policeman, I am afraid. The fear is in this instant, and is therefore a present fear."

But I say this policeman was already settled in memory. Seeing this policeman, you went back to the policeman in memory who did something to scare you. That policeman from the past became this policeman.

Also, while the fear is in this moment, it is fear about the next moment. Will the policeman come and get me? This is now the future, based on the past. There is no difference between past and future. The foundation of the future is the past.

When we speak of living in this present moment, it has nothing to do with the present that is related to past and future. But we have no other word. So don't hold on to the word "present" either. The concept of present must also be transcended.

Transcend name and form. Transcend the light also. Only then will you transcend the present itself.

***

Time is mind. Fear is time. Whenever there is fear, there is time. What we are speaking of is neither time nor mind nor fear. You never touch time; you never touch mind; you never touch fear. Fear is only in duality. Where there are two, there is fear. When you are your Self, there is no fear and you are aloneness. You never touch anything else. Time doesn't touch; mind doesn't touch; fear doesn't touch. You are beyond all that.

All these are concepts. Fear is removed by understanding. Duality is removed by the wisdom of unity. Duality is only in dreaming. When you wake up, nothing else existed. That is total freedom.

This instant of time is beyond the concept of time. Therefore, questions disappear. That is your home, your final abode, where nothing appears. Nothing can touch it.

This is the knowledge of the unknown, which is empty. Nothing is there. No wants, no needs, no desire. This is peace. This is your own Self.

You don't have to attain it, achieve it, or acquire it by any method whatsoever, described by any man or any god or any creator. No effort is needed to reach there. It is the easiest of all to know who you are. You don't need to travel to find freedom. You are already free.

***

Anything that can be rejected, reject it, including this sentence. What's left?

Do not accept any word or speech. All my words are fingers pointing to that unknown which I cannot describe.

Reject my words and you will see what is there for you to see.

***

I find myself getting caught in the greed that I've missed something, that there is something more I haven't got.

This greed is welcome. It will not cling to any object. It is greedy only to measure the fathomlessness. This engagement could be carried on up to the end of your life span, and you will be happy to do this. Not seeking, but intention for deeper peace. This can be kept and there is no problem. You can't get out of this. Always the engagement will remain. This is peace itself.

When you have true peace, you will desire to see if there is even deeper peace. This is Selfward, not outward. You will always like to love more, if you get involved with this love. It is an unending search in the direction of the unknowable.

I don't advise you to stop it. This activity is in the direction of inactivity. It is activity within inactivity. Only joy will be there—beginning, middle, and end. This joy is your nature. It is not searching for something else.

THE GURU

What is the relationship to the man who shows you the rope?

This is the finger pointing to the moon. If you only see the finger, you will miss the moon.

Sometimes there is a desire to have the man walk along with us to point out the snakes and ropes.

You must go alone. All alone. No one can do it for you. This way is not a beaten track where you can be led by someone else. You don't need any help and there is no track. All beaten tracks are the past. Do away with all tracks, all paths, and have no one to lead. All tracks are merely imagination of past and future. Remove all imagination of past and future, and where do you stay?

***

What about all these gurus that do harm?

Yes. There are two sects. How many sheep, how many goats, how many pigs and water buffalo do you see? That is one sect. And how many lions have you seen on your trip here in India? That is the other sect. As long as there are sheep, there will be herders. How many lions do you see being herded?

***

Is obedience to the teacher a way of dealing with ego and personal desire?

Yes. The tradition prescribes that. To ward off the ego you have to have obedience to the teacher. And this teacher is none other than your own Self. You have to be obedient to that which you are seeking.

However, a true teacher does not expect obedience from anybody!!

If you have ego, it has to be brought down to surrender to a higher authority. If you have no ego, there is no need to be obedient to anybody. If you need help erasing this monster, you must turn to a higher authority to take care of this ego. If you have no ego, you need no teacher. The teacher must be your own Self.

But when you ask this question, I think you refer to some preacher, not teacher. A teacher is one who is enlightened himself, and enables another to be enlightened. If there is a candle, it has a flame, and any other candle that touches this flame will be enlightened, just like the candle it touches. If a teacher doesn't give you enlightenment, he is a preacher, not a teacher.

It is so difficult to find a teacher these days. There are mostly preachers. A real teacher has no teaching. He merely apprises you of the fact that you are no different from himself, the Self! You are already that! What is there to teach? The teacher tells you that you are already that. A teacher should be able to allow you to know that you are That itself and to not seek anything anywhere. You are already that! You are already free! The ultimate truth is that there is no teacher, no teaching, and no student.

***

Within this dream of differences, why do some people seem to have the power to transmit the Self-nature and others don't?

Difference from whose side? From the one who transmits or the one who receives the transmission?

When I come here, I sit with you and feel something. When people sit with me, they may not feel anything.

The man to whom this power of transmission is attributed is empty. His mind is empty. Where there is fire, there is naturally heat. But fire does not know it is hot. People go near the man with the empty mind, and their desire will be fulfilled. He may not know. If he knows, it will not be done. Only in the presence of a man who has no desire will the desire be fulfilled.

***

You speak of a razor's edge. We can't really slip off this razor's edge; it is actually just an idea, isn't it?

The sharpest idea! Very narrow. Two cannot walk abreast. If you lose balance you will be cut. If you walk on the razor's edge, you should be single-minded. Not between two minds. And if you stop you will be cut. This is the direction that will lead you to nowhere. This is an idea, and here two ideas cannot travel. Then the idea of the sharp razor goes away when it has done its job. This will lead you to immortality.

Welcome the decision to walk on this, throwing all other ideas away. Who will walk on this edge? Very few.

The razor's edge is not to give rise to a thought. This is the razor's edge. Walk and see. Thoughtlessness will lead you to emptiness. Not by understanding or argument, but by being it, throwing yourself into emptiness—nothing short of it. Not understanding or conception, but by jumping into emptiness right now! When you jump into this, you cannot but speak the truth. Instantly you are free. Don't postpone this freedom, and don't make any plans for the future; then it will happen. Planning is a trick of the mind. The thought arises, "I will make a retreat and do it there." Time means postponement.

***

What happens when the guru dies?

The guru never dies. The guru is your own Self within. You seek him outside, and therefore, out of grace, the

Self takes form and manifests as "the guru outside" just to tell you, "I am within you." That is the whole point of a guru. Trust yourself and look within. Guru is that which dispels darkness. The word itself means "that which dispels darkness, one who dispels ignorance."

There are times when I see that we are part of the same continuum.

Yes. That is being. Not seeing. Being. There is no difference.

I wonder why I become afraid when I am feeling so much love.

Fear of too much joy, happiness, freedom, which you have not tasted before. It is a strange taste, a strange kind of love/beauty you have not seen or heard before. Therefore, with a new environment, the mind is not comfortable and returns back. That is called closing. But it brings some taste along with it. Even if the heart seems closed, that taste is quite enough. If you know your heart seems closed, it is really open. If it were closed you would not see that it seems closed. It is in the opening of the heart that you say, "My heart seems closed." You mean, "Previously, my heart was closed."

The thought persists that a free being would have a soft, open feeling all the time.

Closing and opening require a door. There is no door. Only imagination. Look and see if there is a door or lock. If there is no door, how can it be closed?

Fear or thinking is the door.

Yes. Imagination, not reality. How do you remove the imaginary door? Nobody can tell you. There is no way. This is your own imagination.

What about the sensation of tightness?

In the evening you see a snake. In seeing a snake, how does the fear arise in the mind? How do you get rid of the fear? You find a stick or a rock to hit the snake, or you take out a pistol to shoot the snake, isn't that so? All these things will come up in seeing the snake. From the other side, a man comes and says, "What are you doing? Why are you waiting? It is only a rope."

So look at the snake—fear, safety, stick, pistol, stone—movement has stopped. You are not going forward. A man tells you it is a rope. How does the heart open? How has the fear gone? How has the snake disappeared?

When the habit occurs of contraction or knotting, then there is the thought "No, I don't want a knot." Then the thought arises that freedom is not complete because of a sense of inside and outside.

Some like to keep that thought up to the last when the body drops. Freedom is freedom now or when the body drops. Liberation here and now or after the fall of the body—it is the same. Don't prolong it.

***

Each day of satsang with you is like lifetimes of bliss.

Let me tell you what *satsang* means. *Sangha* is association. *Sat* is Self. So, satsang is Self-association. Your association with the Self is the ultimate satsang.

If you do not recognize where the Self is for this association, then find a teacher who is Self-realized. This is the next best to your own.

Keep quiet. Nothing to think. Silence. Just be quiet. In quietness, in silence, the Self arises by itself. This is the best satsang. If you have no confidence in your own Self, then you seek someone. And by chance, if you are honest, if you are sincere and serious, this Self will lead you to some other place where you will meet the very same Self who will tell you, "I am your own Self."

***

Many gurus tell their devotees that they must surrender. Often people give up their jobs and surrender to the guru. They know they are in a dream world, and they want to surrender to something greater than the dream.

This is forced on people by shepherds.

Shepherds?

Shepherds are the leaders of religion. Shepherds herd all the sheep. Only the sheep are herded, not the lions.

Some spiritual teachers put out a strong message that seekers must surrender, let go, and follow the master.

This creates much fuss when shepherds say, "Come to me, I will give you rest." This kind of surrender is not worth believing in. It has benefited no one yet. Every instant of time for millions of years is a thought. This instant of time is empty. Nothing exists and yet nothing is nonexistent. It is this emptiness that I speak of again and again.

What is surrender?

Teachers misinterpret surrender. Surrender is abandoning the concept that "I am bound." This is surrender. When surrender replaces the concept "I am bound," then nothing can be said of what is surrendered to.

***

We have been comfortable in limitation, so we don't touch limitlessness. When someone imposes limitedness on us, we readily agree. Anything you desire to achieve is a limitation. And you don't have to desire limitlessness, because that you already are.

You make frontiers. The idea "I need freedom" constructs a wall between you and freedom. Remove the concept that there is a wall between you and freedom, and what happens? This wall is imagination. You don't have to remove the rubbish of the wall. What happens if you remove this wall, which does not even exist?

You haven't removed anything.

Then who were you, who are you, and who would you be?

***

Poonjaji has the reputation of being very strongly affirmative about people's experiences. Is it valuable to be very affirmative to the person who is tasting of something?

When I respond I am absolutely empty. I don't search for an answer to the question. I am just empty, without thought. Unconcerned with what is going on. The answer comes from emptiness and not from Poonja. Poonja then has no substance. This student is not my concern. The question is not asked to Poonja. To whom is the question addressed? Poonja cannot bestow freedom upon anybody. The question is asked to the unknown.

This is the teaching of non-teaching.

Yes, this is the teaching of non-teaching. The rest is preaching. The teacher has no teaching of his own. The teacher is pushed to speak and has no responsibility for what is spoken. Simply, you live as a free man, an immaculate, empty man. This is the best teaching that one has to give somebody. Sit absolutely quiet. No thought. This teaching is the best teaching, which no one can reject and all can benefit from.

***

Master, I have just returned to your feet after one month away. I know all of this is a dream and that there is no real leaving. So why do I feel such joy, bliss, and overflowing love to be back in your presence?

We are sitting here at the bank of the Ganga. You see her rushing and noisy as she streams past, running always to the sea. And at the Bay of Bengal, the sea comes up to meet her. The sea comes up and takes the form of the Ganga. And they mix. And who can say which is which? And then all is silent.

I have to thank you so very much.

Why thank me? What have I given you? If we give each other something, then we thank each other.

It is all so clear. Now I can see it.

Now you can see it. You have not taken my eyes to see. The eyes are yours, and sight also is yours.

The fear is gone. The fear is gone. The fear to speak is also gone.

Ah.

It was already on my lips a few times. Then there is no question anymore.

Excellent. Good. Thank you.

You have freed us from so many things.

Yes. Your things.

I am happy. All of you are going home victorious. All these years I was going to your door. Now I am eighty years old and not able to go. So I am sorry I have given you the trouble to come here.

***

Is it true that you made the statement "After I die, I will leave the teaching with no footholds to hold on to"?

Why wait until after I die? [*laughs*]

Just as a bird leaves no trail in the sky as it flies, the true teaching leaves no trace in memory. The teaching must have no teacher and no student. If the teaching comes from the past or memory or concept, it is preaching, not teaching. This teaching never was. [*he smiles and looks around the room*] It never will be. [*he pauses and then laughs*] And it never is.

***

Papaji's teachings took different appearances depending on his audience. The first section reveals the pure essence of his transmission. As his popularity grew and the people became more diverse, he started to teach about desire, and the traps and requirements for meeting a true teacher. This second section comes from this period in his work.

WHAT IS ENLIGHTENMENT?

Papaji, what is enlightenment??
Stillness of mind is enlightenment.
***

When you return to your Self, this is called awakening, liberation, freedom. Having known your Self, you know everything.

In this awakening the whole universe is discovered to be within yourself. All universes are within you, and you are the universe.

This is ultimate understanding. Knowing this, you know everything. If you don't know this, you know nothing, regardless of how much information you collect.

Without this knowledge, you are ignorant. Having known the absolute, you are everything—without beginning, middle, end, without birth or death. Here, all fears end.
***

Enlightenment is out of time. It is not waking, sleeping, or dreaming. Just investigate the desire "I want to be free." From which state does this come? This is a transcendental state that comes from nowhere.

***

Papaji, how can I still the mind?

Traditionally, there are two prescribed ways. One is inquiry, which is suitable to very few, very fit people; the other is yoga. Yoga is concentration, meditation, and practice.

For inquiry, first you must be able to discern what is real from what is unreal. This is quite reasonable. Pick up what is real and adhere to it, or reject the unreal or falsehood.

Studying, pilgrimages, and dips in the holy waters are not going to help you. To know all the sutras and holy knowledge, like a parrot, is no help. Nor will gifts, austerities, or charities help.

The most important requirement is the burning desire for freedom. This desire alone is enough. If you have a burning desire for freedom, satsang will come.

What is satsang? Stay quiet. Wherever the mind goes, bring it back to its source. If you are not able to do it yourself, find a perfect teacher.

You must not make a mistake in your choice of teacher. This is a pact between your human life and enlightenment. Don't waste your life with someone who is not competent to deliver the goods.

If you are bent upon freedom, if you must have freedom in this span of life, this year, this month, this day, now—then you must make a choice. The best choice is inquiry. Then the mind is instantly stilled.

Meditation must be permanent. Not a few hours. You must be centered in the reality of the true Self. Self alone is true; all else is falsehood.

You must abandon everything! Finally, abandon the study of any book. Open your own book and keep quiet.

***

Of six billion people in the world, how many desire freedom? How rare is it? It may not be possible for the earth to produce even one enlightened person in a country. To see an enlightened man we look back 2,535 years. We find this prince who became enlightened, and still every day we repeat his name.

When he woke up he was sleeping with his wife—his queen—and his son. He had a palace, elephants, horses, treasures, armies, and dancing girls. This young man had not seen any suffering in the palace. From where did his desire "I want to be free" arise?

At midnight he woke up. On one side he saw the beauty of the land, his wife; on the other side, his son, the gift of married life. This man woke up in between.

As you hear this, don't exclude yourself! You are Buddha yourself. He was a human. You are a human. He had perhaps more responsibilities than you have. His engagements were tremendous, much more than yours. And he had to find time for this desire for freedom.

After finding the time, this man is now showing us the light. He is not dead. We remember him every day. He lives in the heart of everyone. Who does not know Buddha? In each country his name is shining. You are Buddha yourself! Don't underestimate yourself. You have the same light, the same wisdom, the same consciousness, he had.

If you want to postpone, you can go on to the next birth. If you have desires and they are not fulfilled, you have to be reborn into the next womb. If you want to stop it, fulfill all your desires in an instant. If no desires are left, how can you be reborn?

The only way off this circle is to fulfill all your desires in an instant. You've been trying the other way. You fulfill one desire; then another comes. You fulfill it, yet another comes. Ask the kings, the rulers of this world, and you will find they have desires and fears. Ask the businessman. He, too, has desires and fears: he wants more money. The worker, the priest, the soldier—everybody has unfulfilled desires. The simple way to fulfill your desires is with fire. You need fire to burn the storehouse of these desires that you have accumulated in the bag of your memory. Instantly they will be fired by one desire: enlightenment!

In enlightenment, all desires are reduced to ashes. You no longer need to return to any womb. Otherwise, you have to be hitchhiking from place to place, womb to womb.

It doesn't take any time. Just have this one desire. It has to work because this desire can't land on any object. Desires for objects, wanting what you don't have, can take some time. But this desire—to know your own true Self—can't take you far away for its fulfillment.

This desire will be fulfilled instantly, because the desired object is the subject! It is the subject aspiring to return to subject. Consciousness desires, from within consciousness, to return to consciousness. How much time do you need to return home, while sitting at home?

***

From what I understand, we are all enlightened, and we must let go of the concept that we are not enlightened. Is this correct?

Part of it you have understood. "I am not enlightened" is a concept. "I am enlightened" is also a concept. Have you understood? Get rid of both these concepts, and what do you see?

[*silence*]

Aha. This smile on your face is neither enlightened nor bound. Keep smiling, and keep quiet. When you smile, what thought is in your mind? Who are you? Who is smiling? By rejecting bondage and freedom, there is smiling. Now you proceed, without referring to bondage or enlightenment.

***

Papaji, I have been sitting here for several days now, and I ask questions, but every time you look at me, I don't know what happens. I don't understand a word you are saying. It is as if you are speaking a foreign language. Should I make an effort to understand?

You can make an effort if you like. Who is to stop you? Even this thought to make an effort must come from source. But before you make this effort, do you need to make an effort to become a man?

No, I am a man.

Like this. So why try to become a horse? [*laughter*]

But I don't understand the words you are speaking. Like right now, as you look at me, something happens, and I don't understand.

You don't need to understand. I will go on talking until your understanding is fulfilled. The end of your understanding will be the end of my talking. So give up understanding, and I'll give up talking also. Understanding will not help. It will go straightaway from the ear to the memory. Understanding may be good for learning something, but not for freedom. For freedom, you do not need a single word. Freedom is immaculate.

***

You say, in sixty years, only a handful of people have come to you and actually realized final freedom. What does this mean about us?

I haven't excluded you from my list. [*laughter*]

***

If this is a dream, why do so many people believe it is real?

No one doubts the reality of the world. They see trees and mountains, and they are certain that all of it exists. Only when this certainty is challenged is the dream doubted. Wake up, and find it was a dream.

How to wake up? By satsang. Satsang is the talk of freedom. By satsang you realize that you can give up all dreams of the body and all these relationships. There are very, very few who actually choose to wake up.

Buddha woke up. He was sleeping with his beautiful young wife, and he woke up. Beautiful wife on one side, son on the other, palace, elephants—and he chose something else.

Another king woke up. He was lying on the roof of his palace, with two queens—one on either side—on a full moon night. He was looking at the beauty of the moon when two white birds flew by. Suddenly he woke up and looked at the situation. A king in his palace, with a queen on either side. He had the maximum the world could offer. What a lucky person! He quietly woke up, left the palace, and went to the forest to live in freedom.

Here and there, you will find different stories of waking up. When you wake up, you will know this was only a dream state. When you are dreaming it all seems real, and you do not know you are dreaming. Finally, the discrimination comes from the question "Where have I come from? Who am I?" With this discrimination you will realize the nature of this dream.

***

What is enlightenment??

I don't use this word.

Realized?

Nothing. Don't become anything. Even enlightenment is becoming something. Be as you are. Don't label yourself. Don't have any brand. Brand is for animals. What brand can there be for the Self, which has no name and no form! What is the source of the word "enlightenment"? It is a word, isn't it? Before it was a word, what was the source of the root of this word?

It is a thought.

Yes, and before thought, it was silence. So, first silence, then thought, then words. "Enlightenment" and "bondage" are words. All words are in the realm of the mind, and you are opening to that which is beyond mind.

Before becoming a thought, it was somewhere else, and this somewhere else is your own Self.

Self is always Self; let it not be branded. Self is Self, and does not need your effort or method or help to realize itself. It is ever-realized. On the contrary, you are camouflaging it. That camouflage must be removed.

What is the camouflage? Camouflage is the thought "I am so-and-so." That has to be removed, and when it goes, Self is self-effulgent. It shines by its own shine on itself. To remove the camouflage, you don't need any practice. Just keep quiet for an instant, and all is over, and you are at home.

Hearing the words in your presence, something happens.

Yes, it is happening. Because of silence, quietness, and peace. Absolute silence. When the mind is quiet it is called presence, and this presence is very contagious. Everyone who comes into its orbit is affected. Quietness of mind is most important, not thoughts, not words. You don't need words to teach. Just keep quiet.

This teaching doesn't need any words. Just quiet mind. And since nobody is quiet, the teachings aren't working. There are millions of books, but nothing is working because the mind behind the writing is not quiet. Some sutras are quite effective because they were written by a silent mind.

The word rises from silence before it is a word. So speak in silence; hear in silence. For freedom you don't need a word. Freedom is transmitted in silence.

REQUIREMENTS FOR SATSANG

There are certain qualifications to be fulfilled before one goes to a teacher for freedom.

The first requirement, discernment, is discrimination between what is real and what is unreal. This distinction is essential. You must desire what is real and reject what is unreal. What is real can only be truth. Your own Self. There is nothing beyond this. All the rest is falsehood.

The second requirement is to rid yourself of desire for pleasures of the senses.

The third qualification is to abandon physical and mental karma.

The fourth qualification is to desire freedom intensely.

Look at the few who have woken up, and you will see they have fulfilled these requirements and demands.

With these qualifications, you are ready to sit with a teacher. A perfect teacher is one who has realized himself.

Only being with a perfect teacher is worthwhile.

As the moneychanger tests his gold, you have every right to test your teacher. Don't be misled. When you go to the supermarket, you choose what to buy. Why not be even more careful in choosing a teacher?

This is the age of Kali Yuga [Age of Darkness]. There can be falsehood everywhere. Most teachers are false teachers, and most seekers are false seekers.

Many say, "I want freedom," but qualifications have to be met before one receives satsang.

Since you are here, I will assume that you have discernment. As for the second condition, rejection of desires, I do not even ask you about abandonment of pleasures. Some people are in favor of committing all sorts of sensual pleasures, and I don't think they will be successful. Can you tell me any person involved in sense pleasures who has become enlightened?

As to karma, let me tell you a story so you won't be confused about living in the world and karma. There was a teenage princess who desired to be free. She decided to go see a saint who lived in a thatched hut on the outskirts of town. Nobody knew what she was doing. In the night when everyone was sleeping, she would get up and slip out to spend an hour with the saint.

One of her brother's friends said, "I see your sister in the night. Where does she go?"

The brother said, "She doesn't go anywhere. She sleeps here."

But the brother stayed awake to watch. At midnight he saw his sister slip away and head out of town. He followed her with a gun. He felt that if she was seeing someone, he would kill them both with a single shot.

As she entered the hut the sage brightened the light and said, "Come, sit in front of me. Today is the final day. Today I will transmit freedom to you."

Meanwhile, outside, the brother saw his sister inside the hut with a strange man. True to his purpose, he took aim. The brother was not a seeker. He went for a different purpose than his sister.

He aimed to have both in the same shot.

The guru uttered a secret word, given from teacher to disciple in strictest confidence. When the secret enters the nerves of the disciple, all is over. The guru uttered the word, and someone outside started dancing! The saint reprimanded the girl for bringing someone. She defended her innocence, saying she didn't bring anyone.

"Then go and see who is dancing in ecstasy." She went out and found her brother. They embraced, and he fell at her feet to thank her.

Simply by keeping good association and listening to the word, the miracle happened. The brother was not qualified in the traditional sense. In aiming he had no other desire except to shoot both of them. He aimed one-pointedly at enlightenment, and the result was ecstasy and gratefulness.

Your associations must reflect external purity. This is absolutely essential. External purity goes with internal purity. Internal purity is the intense desire for freedom.

***

Respect is essential. If you have a diamond, don't keep it in a plastic bag. You must have a wrapping equal to its preciousness. This is respect. You must be humble to all beings. If you are not, you are arrogant.

Everybody is arrogant at first. No one is humble. It is not your fault. The ego is arrogance, and this serpent has bitten all the beings of the world. All are arrogant, even gods.

If you feel you are arrogant, satsang is the place to remove it. It is very simple.

The foundation of arrogance is the thought "I am the body." "This is mine, and I want that." "I belong to this." "This belongs to me." All these thoughts display arrogance.

Most human beings are involved in this arrogance. That is why satsang cannot work for them. When you are arrogant, you conceal your own Self-nature of beauty, bliss, and freedom. You can't have peace when you are arrogant.

If you are truly ready to get rid of arrogance, come to satsang, approach a teacher very humbly, and ask, "Sir, how to remove the arrogance?"

***

Even to say, "I am arrogant," is humility itself.

Who says, "I am arrogant," first of all? Have you ever heard anyone say, "I am arrogant"? Everyone says, "You are arrogant."

When you are arrogant, peace and bliss are hidden. When you realize peace and bliss, arrogance hides. So fall in love with peace.

Find out who you really are, and arrogance will be removed. You will meet your divine nature itself, here and now. Don't stir a thought! Don't make any effort and there is no arrogance. If you pick up a thought, "I have done that, and this belongs to me. Tomorrow I will have..."—all these thoughts are arrogance!

You can do nothing. Nothing is in your hand. Incessantly inquire, "Who am I?" Keep your mind here.

What you think, so you are now. What your thought is, so your being is.

If your thought is empty, there is no reason for the next birth.

***

Never-ending eternal satsang is already going on, from before this cosmos, and it will remain after the destruction of the world. Beauty reveals herself in satsang.

But whosoever is arrogant will not get a glimpse. Whoever is arrogant cannot see it, because this love, this beauty, is so immaculate, so chaste, so virginal, that even a thought to see it is an impediment to realizing it.

So you have to go as chaste as It is. As nude, as immaculate, as virginal, as It is. Then you present yourself. Oneness, beauty, and love meeting oneness, beauty, and love.

There is no one to be seen, felt, or spoken to. This is satsang. Not even oneness, let alone twoness. Not even oneness. Then satsang takes place.

***

If you are a sharp-witted person, one word in satsang is quite enough. Satsang is not for dull, wicked people.

It is for a very sharp, very sincere, very pure, very holy person.

Truth exalts a holy person. This is truth. No compromise. It is truth that is going to pick you up. It is truth that is going to embrace you. You have to become so beautiful that it will kiss you.

A single fault and you are not worthy of being hugged and kissed. It is immaculate. Truth is going to be your lover. Don't hide. Don't hide anything.

If you are going to be engaged anywhere else, how will your lover pick you up? If you are in a red-light district, you cannot have this immaculate relationship with your own Self.

***

In many places in this world, if you declare you are free they stone you to death. The Sufi Mansoul was stoned to death for saying, "I am free."

You are lucky to belong to your country. You must have great merit to have been born in a free land where you can do whatever you want. You can live as you like. You can walk out on the church, and no one questions you.

There are countries where you can't leave the church. There are whole countries where no one would dare to say, "I want to be free."

You have lucky inheritance, lucky parents, lucky country, lucky lineage, and you are lucky yourself. You have this desire for freedom. What more merit do you need? Only look within for an instant and see what is there.

RELATIONSHIP TO THE TEACHER

Traditionally, the student goes to the teacher in the forest and says, "Please, master, save me. I am suffering. Tell me, who am I?"

With all love, the teacher says, "My dear son, come sit here and I will tell you."

Then inquiry starts. The student asks, "Who am I?" and the teacher tells you the truth: "You are That!"

He speaks the truth, and the student understands: "I am That."

And it is finished.

***

What is a teacher?

A teacher is a raft to ferry you across to the other side of the ocean. A true teacher carries you across the ocean of samsara.

The snapping alligators and crocodiles in this ocean are your desires. Is there any desire that will not swallow you up? Some time, some day, that alligator of desire will swallow you. The whole world is being devoured by these alligators of attachment and desire.

Free your mind of all attachment, and you are God itself. Free of desire, you are absolute. There is no doubt about it. Just get rid of desire for one second, and see how you feel.

In this instant, you fall in love with your own Self. You cannot find peace in any object. Stop rushing toward any object, and see. The whole world is rushing toward objects in search of peace. It cannot be found in any objects. Stop your race and see.

***

How is it possible that you give this rarest of all precious gems to anyone who walks in the door?

Thirty years ago my mother used to ask the same thing. She would say, "Look, you are spreading pearls before swine. Who values what you are giving?"

She said, "You must first evaluate a person. Look at all the swamis. People spend their whole life serving them in the ashram, and the swami gives nothing because he has nothing. Immediately these people come, and you are giving away pearls. Who knows the value of this?"

"Beware," she said. "See the quality of a person, and then give him what he needs. In this way the diamond need not be tied around the donkey's neck. You must evaluate. Only then you will know."

But what to do? I believe a human birth is enough. There are only six billion humans. Count the mosquitoes or the fishes, the worms or the germs. Human birth is rare and lucky enough to recognize the true gem.

***

Sometimes I am aware—

Sometimes! What do you mean by "sometimes"? It is not good grammar. Where did you learn this? What school did you go to learn this? Who were your teachers? This is a different class! This is a class where there is no teacher, a teacher has no tongue, and the students have no heads on their shoulders. This is that class.

If you have a head, you have to go somewhere else. Go perhaps to some butchery where heads are beheaded.

Ego is a head, you see. Ego is birth heading toward the butchery. The butchers will take care of you very well. I don't want heads. I want hearts.

There are many institutions that need only the head. I don't need any head to come here. Remove your head outside and then speak. Your heart will speak. You will speak the language of love. Allow your heart to speak. Don't interfere. Let it speak.

You are speaking from the head. Behead it!

***

A beautiful story came into my mind, of Saint Kabir. He had a seven-year-old daughter. One day she asked, "Father, five or six hundred people come to you every day for satsang. Why do they come? What is their purpose?"

Kabir replied, "They are coming for satsang. In search of truth. To have freedom. To have wisdom, emancipation."

The young girl said, "I do not believe this is so, my dear Papa. I don't believe they are coming for enlightenment."

Kabir kept quiet.

The next day the little girl stood outside. As each person approached, she said, "Today my father has decided first to interview you. After your interview, he will call you inside."

She continued, "That is why I am here. I have a very sharp chopper in my hand. Put your head down on this log of wood, and I will chop it off. I will show it to my father. After this interview, if he approves, you will be called in."

Everyone in the satsang line was silent.

The first man finally said, "No, no. We are only here to fix the engagement of our daughter. We had some time, so we just came to have the guru's blessings. So we salute, and we go."

Another group came. They only had some lawsuit which needed the guru's advice. Another wanted advice on how to deal with a marriage partner. Others only wanted to know what the guru thought about how to solve their personal or business relationships.

Like this, with some pretext or another, no one was ready to lie down and present his head to the teacher.

Time passed, and still Saint Kabir was waiting, but no one came. Finally he went outside and asked his daughter why no one came in to satsang.

She answered, "I told them that my father wanted to interview them first. I told them I would chop off their heads and bring them in for the interview. Nobody would enter! No one dared!"

"Nobody presented his head! Nobody lay down! Nobody allowed me to chop off his head. So what's the use of your satsang, Papa?"

Every body has to die. From the day of the body's birth, death is just following behind. If they had lain down to be beheaded, they would have realized the truth of who dies! They would know then what life is! No one agreed to live!

This little seven-year-old girl knew how to attend satsang.

These *I's* and *you's* and *me's* and *he's* and *she's* are not allowed in satsang. You are about to see truth face-to-face. That is the meaning of satsang. You are facing truth, freedom, your own Self.

Who can kill you? You are afraid of your own Self, and you depend upon other selves. You depend upon matters which are not permanent. *I* and *you* will not save your life. Millions of times you have been born, and millions of times you have been dead.

You know this taste of death very well. Now at least start to know how to live. You can't save your life. Your body is born to die. You like dying. Millions of times you have experienced death, so you like death. You don't like to live!

It's so simple to live. So simple to be happy, so simple to be always in bliss. And you simply want death; that's all. You are converting this love garden of grace and beauty into a butchery.

Allow some time, just a moment, to see who you are. Allow time to your Self. You never allow time to your own Self. You have been using your head for a million years. Now at least give time to your true heart.

Keep quiet. Simply keep quiet, and you will know what happens. Now, in this very instant, keep quiet. Put your tools down. Your own Self will come and hug you and kiss you.

Allow it. Allow this instant to your own Self.

***

Do not listen to this teaching with your ears. If you do, it will go straightaway into the storehouse of the graveyard. Isn't memory a graveyard? What else is the memory? Are not the dead cobs stored in memory?

Whatever is fresh is not found in memory. In memory you cannot smell anything but trash. All corpses have passed to there. Therefore, forget about it. Don't do anything and don't think anything. That's all.

This is the only teaching. It is not for you to hear. Don't hear anything. Don't listen, don't see, don't smell, don't touch, don't taste anything, and then what is left with you?

Open the heart. That's all.

***

Throughout India people go on pilgrimages. Once a man from the north became friends with a pilgrim from the south, and they stayed at each other's house on their journeys.

The friend from the south said, "I am a wealthy man. We live very well. I have two boys in school, and if they knew how much we had, they would not finish school. So I have hidden a treasure under my wife's millstone. When my sons are finished with school, I will divide the wealth between the boys and my wife."

Seven years passed, and again the man from the north came to visit his friend in the south. He was very surprised to see the shabby condition of the house. Then he saw that his friend's wife looked very unhappy. She was milling her neighbor's wheat.

The friend asked, "What has happened here?"

The wife said, "Six years ago my husband went to the forest and was bitten by a snake and died. Since then life has been very hard for us."

"The boys are just finishing school. They have taken their final examinations. As soon as they are out of school, maybe they can find work to help me."

"Since my husband's death I have been taking in my neighbors' washing. I clean their houses; I grind their flour. And still we don't have enough to eat."

"Didn't your husband tell you anything before he died?"

"No," she said. "His death was quite sudden. We did not get to speak."

The friend was very excited to inform her, "Under the mill that you are grinding, he has hidden a treasure of gold coins."

On simply hearing this information from a reliable authority, she stopped grinding. She stopped what she was doing and immediately became very happy.

The treasure had not even been dug up. After merely hearing the information from a reliable authority, she was convinced. She became very happy.

Now I tell you to remove the suffering. Dig six inches under the suffering, and the treasure is already there. This family was suffering and grinding merely because it did not have the correct information.

This information is from someone who is very close. He says, "There is a treasure, a treasure within you!"

Go inside and you will find it. This is not even a finding. It has always been there. But it has been covered with ignorance. Now it can be discovered based only upon the information of someone who knows. He tells you to remove the suffering and look under the suffering. There is the treasure. Instantly everyone discovers richness.

The treasure is there, but true information is lacking. You simply don't know it. So you go to your neighbors to wash their laundry. And this laundry is memory. When you know the treasure is waiting, instantly you stop going to your neighbors to wash. Otherwise, all you do is laundry.

***

Over thousands of years it is the same. Here and there, you will find a very few true teachers where people are benefited. What is happening here is in that tradition, that lineage. It has always been this way.

If there is a mass, a crowd, take it for granted that there is some fraud going on as well. Some crowd or some traffic jam—there must be some accident. A few people—two, three, or four—is quite enough.

If some dance was going on in the road, how many of you would stay here in satsang? Be honest. Music, dance—so attractive to the senses—and you are gone. Senses are outgoing. Touching, tasting, looking, hearing. Some big attraction outside and you are gone. Who would stay here in satsang? Let alone, who would come to his own Atman, his own Self?

***

When I sit in your presence, everything dissolves.

Presence is always there. Being with Being is enough. Before, you were interested in becoming. Being is presence, and to recognize this is wisdom and freedom.

There is something that happens in your presence. Would you call it grace?

Grace and presence, same thing.

Does one need a guru?

Your Self is your guru, but you have not seen him within you. You do not understand the language of this guru within you. If you are very serious, if you have a longing, a burning desire, to see him, what he does is introduce you to someone who has your same tongue to speak to you.

The inner Self takes the form of the guru without, to speak to you in your lisping tongue. He tells you, "I am within you."

When this outer guru is recognized as your Self, you will understand.

Separation is ego and must be surrendered. In this separation, ego is subject and God is object.

A wave imagines herself to be independent from the sea. She has a different name, a different form and movement, and doesn't see the ocean out of which she is born. This is ego.

Then someone tells you, "You belong to the ocean. You are always the ocean." The ocean is the subject.

But it is more than just telling. My experience is not that you tell me, but that your being is that, and it transmits itself so that I directly experience it. Then I know we are not separate.

This is grace. This is presence. This is divinity speaking. Everything you will see is the same. The eyes will be so divinized they will see only the divine.

As you speak, I look in your eyes and I directly experience, as the words come, that I am speaking to my Self.

Yes. Same Self. The absolute exalts a holy person. When you see the same person, your own Self, this is holiness. Same one speaks and same one hears. When you surrender to the divine, it is the divine which looks out through your eyes. The divine is looking.

***

Who is graced with grace?
Everybody.
Everybody has it?
Yes, everybody has it.
Why do so few people hear it?
Those few know that they have it. Others don't.
Why are they chosen?
Grace from within chooses you. The Self, within itself, the source of this

grace, is so kind to you. It needs to speak to you in your own tongue. It takes you to a person who appraises you of this fact. He will speak to you in your own tongue, and he will only tell you that you are free already. Anybody who tells you to do this or that should not be called a teacher. They may be called a butcher.

A butcher?

Yes, what else? A teacher releases you from all activity, all concepts and burdens.

For thirty-five million years you have been doing. When you finally reach a true teacher, he will not ask you to do anything. He will say, "My dear son, just come and sit quietly. Be quiet. That's all. Don't do anything."

The guru within is your own Self from within. But you don't know him; you don't recognize him. You don't understand his language of silence, so he will introduce you to someone who will speak something and ask you to keep quiet. This is grace. This is your own grace. It comes from within you. Who else can give you this?

But it's not mine. I don't own it.

No, it's not yours. When you say it's not yours, it is not of the body. It is neither within nor without.

***

After being here, I feel you are in my heart. I recognize you as my teacher, as a master. I want to humbly ask that you accept me as a student.

To whom are you asking the question?

The one who sits before me and inside me.

Go to the heart right now. No time to waste. Heart is very near. How far is the heart from you?

No distance.

So go there immediately, and what answer do you get? Mind you, there duality does not exist. [*silence*]

This is the answer. Duality does not exist when you return to your heart, and this heart is another name for truth, reality, freedom. Look within, and approach with all devotion unto your own heart.

There is only space and quiet.

This is the teacher, and this is the teaching. Stay as your heart; that's all. [*laughs*] Stay as your heart.

THE NATURE OF I

There may be one thousand mirrors, each reflecting a different reflection of the sun. There are not one thousand suns. There is one sun shining in all. Reflections may be different. Sun is the same. Sun is one, shining in everything, in every atom. Same.

Consciousness is the same. It may appear to be a bird, or animal, or tree, or rock, or human. When you realize that, you will not suffer. You will enjoy. You don't need anything when you are total. This is absolute, total, complete, perfect. All emptiness. All consciousness.

Don't give rise to the notion *I,* and instantly you will see who you are. You will live very well.

What is your experience now?
Emptiness.
And what rises from emptiness and returns to emptiness?
Emptiness!
Yes. Very good. So when you use the word "I," refer to total emptiness. Then there will be no identification with falling or rising. You will know very well,

"It is within me. All the cosmos rises and falls in me." Where is sorrow or suffering when all the cosmos rises and falls in you?

***

Someone asks, "Who are you?"

If your answer is, "I am Nicholson," "I am Thompson," "I am Wolfgang," and so on, then you really do not know the answer to this question.

Simply ask yourself, "Who am I?"

Usually, when you identify yourself, you refer to your body for the answer. How have you become what changes?

Childhood came and now is gone. Change. You say, "When I was a child ... I was playing ... I went to school."

Then youth came. No more childhood. Same person became a young man. You say, "I was a youth, with new responsibilities..."

Now youth is also gone. Next comes old age. You have had the experience of childhood and youth, but old age does not give you experience to look back upon. You cannot say, "When I was old..." Old age will take you away.

What changes? The body changes. Childhood to youth. Youth to old age. Old age to disease, and disease to death. And that ends this round.

You, however, remain the same. "When I was a child..." "When I was a young man..." "When I am an old man..." The *I* remains the same. And *I* is the same one in everybody! Everybody says "I."

The bodies are different. The *I* is the same. There is one absolute reality in all beings that does not change.

So identify with that which does not change. Not with what is born and dies. How have you, the changeless, identified with that which changes? Identify yourself not with the body, which changes, but with *I*.

For all these years, generation after generation, you have been identifying this *I* with the body, with the mind, with the ego, with the senses, and with manifestation. You have not been told to know, "Who is this *I*?"

It is so simple. What does not change is immortal truth, is eternal happiness, is bliss, is consciousness and existence which has no change. So how is it possible that instead of identifying yourself as eternal happiness, you identify with that which changes, suffers, and dies, time and again?

We have come together to find out how to get rid of the identification with that which changes, and to identify with that which is changeless and will remain changeless. What difficulty can there be? Simply give a patient reasoning, once, at any time: now in this life, or in the next life.

You are not going to be happy unless you solve this question. And perhaps this question has never confronted you. You have always been asking questions to others. And others have been asking questions to you. But this question has never occurred. And this question, perhaps, will be the answer itself!

But you must be serious. If you fail to solve this question, what is lacking is only sincerity.

At the age of seventeen, my teacher left his home. No practice, no study. When I met him years later, he said, "You are God itself. You are God."

And I didn't have any doubt about it. It is a matter of minutes between a student who is really qualified, deserving, obedient, and a perfect teacher. You don't need any practice. How far can your Self be away from you? How far is *I* situated from you that you need any kind of practice to get there? If it was away, then, of course, you would need some vehicle, by air or road or surface. But it is within. Within the within. Nearer than your breath. From where the breath arises.

What do you need to do? Only give up your effort. You need effort to get hold of something. You need effort to imagine something. But, for this, you don't need to imagine anything, because it is the fountain from where the imagination itself arises. From where the thought itself arises, what can you think about? Therefore, you are not to think. And you are not to do any kind of practice, or travel, or fix any destination.

First remove all these imaginations. Let your intention be of a different order from the intention to practice or to postpone; then wipe out everything that comes into your mind, including the ideas about freedom or enlightenment, or even what you are searching for. Not even the concept of search may arise in your mind. This freedom from your ideas of yourself is what I speak about!

Nobody else can give you anything. This is your own affair. And you have to do it yourself. Even if you postpone, if you postpone for millions of years—at the end of millions of years, you are going to get it.

When you know, you realize there has been no sleep at all, no ignorance, no darkness. When there is light, where is the darkness? When there is knowledge, where is the ignorance? When there is a rope, where is the snake? When there is no misunderstanding, where is the mirage? All creations of the mind. And you have created it all yourself, due to the imagination.

What is that imagination? "I am not that. I am not absolute freedom. I am not absolute existence." You are identifying yourself with something that is not abiding, that is not changeless, that is not eternal. This is the postponement.

This postponement is like a grinding mill; day and night, it is grinding. The grinding mill is working, and all the beings are being crushed like grains. The mill is working, the stones are moving, and beings are being crushed.

A few here and there—one or two—may be safe near the center pivot, where nothing can crush them. Anything which is away from the center, the Self, the absolute existence, has to be crushed.

***

This awareness without subject or object must be discovered. This is your own awareness, and it is called freedom from everything.

I arises and behaves as if it is awareness. Ego and the world arise, and the ego separates itself from the Self and calls itself self-sufficient. All trouble arises from this. This ego arises from awareness and behaves as if it is separate from awareness. [*laughs*]

It takes responsibility on its shoulders and gives no peace, no happiness, no joy. Instead, you search for happiness in object after object in time. All these notions arise from the wrong notion of *I*.

When you search for this *I*, it disappears, leaving pure awareness. Not "I am aware," nor awareness of any object. No subject. No object. No day and no night. No duality. No opposites. This is ultimate knowledge. Without this, everyone is creating samsara. To stay here is to help everyone.

This must be realized before helping anyone else. This knowledge is compassion. Nothing more than this. It cannot be done by doing anything, reading anything, or practicing anything. It is whatever it has been. This knowledge is ultimate knowledge. Not by any doing. If you do anything, it will be called a gain or attainment by some process. Any practice will be physical or mental. This does not depend on any mind or any body. Anything that rises from here, it is that!

This knowledge reveals by itself. It is always here—omnipresent, omniscient, eternal peace—everybody's Self-nature. It is here, and you are putting your head someplace else. Therefore, I say, "Keep quiet." Let it reveal itself to itself. It doesn't need any help. It is self-effulgent. It shines by its own light. It doesn't need anybody's candle.

***

You say, inquire "Who am I?" But you also say it cannot be done with words or mind. Could you explain?

Yes. Even parrots can be taught to say, "Who am I? Who am I? Who am I?" The inquiry I speak of is Self with the Self.

It is because of the misidentification of the Self that it thinks it is not the Self. In consciousness, there arises some doubt in the mind of consciousness that "I am not consciousness."

This doubt is like a wave arising in the ocean of consciousness. What is needed for this thought to return back to the ocean, since it already is that ocean?

***

Sometimes the *I* and the thoughts rise up.

When the *I* falls into the ocean, this is what has been waited for. Then there is no more *I*. Return to the ocean as the ocean; then there is no more *I*.

The ocean is dancing. Seeing is dancing. This is a total *I*. One *I* is a spurious *I*, egoistic *I*. There is also another *I*. Ocean is total *I*.

I means total *I*. Ocean as waves. *I* am waves. *I* am rising and *I* am falling. From ocean's view, ocean is rising and ocean is falling.

Give up your identification with the individual *I* that you had been using before. When that *I* is there, there are others also: *I, you,* and *he.*

This *I* is total *I* when there is no difference between the waves and ripples and bubbles and tides. All is one ocean. *I* has no notion, no separation, no individuality, from ocean. This can be a very beautiful dance, if one understands. This is total consciousness.

***

How do I stop trying?

First find out who is trying. "Who is trying?" points you to the Self. Right now! Find the person who is trying.

I am trying.

Okay, "I am trying." Return back, "I am trying." "Trying" returns to *am*, and *am* returns to *I*. Now you are at *I*. Now tell me, who is trying?

Look behind the *I*. Look underneath the *I*. Look for the source of *I*. Now tell me where the *I* rises from; who is trying? "Trying am I" returns you back from where you came. Look underneath. Look at the very source from where the *I* is springing. Look down. You said, "How do I stop trying?" Look at the source of the *I* that is trying.

I'm confused.

Look at the source of *I*, and what confusion is there?

None.

None. Okay, so now you are at the source of *I*. Tell me, is there any confusion?

No.

What else is there? Then tell me, who is trying? You stay here for some time and look around where there is no

I and watch for the thought "I am trying." Look around.

I am looking and I can't see anything.

See the source of *I*. Where does it arise from?

Here.

Okay, here. Be in the here itself and see what to do. You look around and see who is here, present in the here!

No one.

Then who is trying?

Nobody.

Nobody is trying. If you are nobody, then nobody's trying. Then what is the trouble with you? [*laughter*]

Let nobody try. Let nobody try, and let nobody die, and what does it matter to you? What does it matter? Let nobody try and let nobody die. You have no problem. How is the climate here now? Does it suit you? [*laughter*]

Nobody's there.

If nobody is there, this is peace. If any body trespasses, then that peace is disturbed. When no thing is there, when no body is there, when you are all alone—not even a thought—what do you call this state: agitation or peace?

Peace.

What did you do to get peace, since a moment before you were agitated?

I looked.

Yes. You haven't looked before; therefore, you were agitated. After millions of years of agitation, you look and you find peace. Look again. Come on. Look again, again look. Travel with me for some time.

Now I can see the face. This is not an agitated face now. Excellent, excellent. For so long she has been waiting for you. Where have you been wandering?

***

The best way to see an enlightened man is to be enlightened yourself. You may have no right to ask about anyone else, but every right to ask, "Who am I?"

What about compassion for others? Doesn't compassion need two?

Does your stomach thank your hands for bringing food to your mouth? When you say "I," do you think of all the individual hairs on your body? Does having two arms and two legs mean the body is in parts, or is it one body?

For the stomach to thank the mouth implies otherness. To have a concept of compassion also implies otherness. Hands are not compassionate to stomach. When you "know" that this is compassion, it is not compassion. It is then the teaching of the missionaries. How to act compassionate. How the hands should be. This is the mischief that religions preach. They preach fear and punishment before death and heaven after death.

***

You are not to understand it by the mind. Just keep quiet. Let it arise itself. Keep quiet. See that no thought touches you for this moment. And you are here—always here.

What if the question is, "Why am I?"

It amounts to the same thing.

Same thing. [doubtfully] How...?

Stress is on the *I.* It all resolves back to the *I.* "Who" and "what" merge into the *I* itself.

"Who" and "what" maybe, but "why"?

"What" and "who" and "why" are born from the *I* itself. Their mother is *I*. So now question to the mother itself. Find the mother itself, *I* itself.

Look to where the mother is born. You are born from the mother; "what" and "why" are born from this same mother, *I*. Look to where this mother was born: look to grandmother. Where has this mother taken birth? For the mother, you have to go to your grandmother.

How to find the grandmother, how to find the source? Just give up the effort. Just give up effort of any sort, physical or mental or whatever.

So I turn toward the source?

No. Source is already there. Just inquire what the *I* is. When you inquire under the *I*, it disappears. When it disappears, it went to see its source; and having a dip into the source, this *I* has become no-*I*.

The question is: What is this no-*I* from where everything arises? Everything is there. Would-be things are there also. Waves would be there in the serene, waveless ocean. The potentiality is there for waves to arise that are not there now. And you are that. Identify and merge into the water and the wave.

Water has to merge into wave, and wave has to merge into water, because they are the same. Water and wave are not different. Ocean and water are not different. Emptiness and consciousness are not different. And you and consciousness are not different. You must be conscious of your own Self.

When you are conscious of the mountain, the trees, the grass, the donkey—are not all of these within your consciousness? All this is consciousness. Everything is consciousness, and you are that consciousness. How do you differ from anybody else? Who are the others? Where are the others, in consciousness?

There is no difference.

Yes, difference is only a fancy of the mind. Actually no difference.

So truly your question is the best question—"Who am I?"—because it is a subjective question. All other questions are objective questions.

There is a subjective question that nobody asks. Everyone asks, "Who are you? Who is he?" Nobody has time to ask, "Who am I?" Nobody.

He who questions is free from this manifestation, free of this cycle of birth and death forever. And there are very few people who inquire into their own Self. The rest don't; therefore, they will suffer.

Few here and there have taken the step to inquire, taken the courage to inquire. It is not knowing, receiving, achieving, or attaining anything. Just realization. Discover. You have to discover; that's all.

Bliss is already here, and you are begging.

***

When there is illusion, substance is hidden by name and form. You say your name is Susan. You think, "I look like this. My form is this. My age is this. I belong to this country. I belong to this sex."

This body is form, and Susan is the form's name. This conceals the reality.

Wherever there is name and form, there is falsehood. They are not permanent.

In sleep, these names and forms don't go with you. So ask this question: "Without name and form, who am I?"

Beyond name and form, which are not real, who are you? You are not this dress, these earnings, or this hair. You are not the body! You are not the mind!

What's left? It's already here. Being is left and non-being is wiped out. Being is here; beauty is here; eternity is here. And That is what you are.

***

Everyone is sleeping. When you see other, when you see otherness, when you see duality, it is called dreaming. Only in the dream do you see objects. When there is other, it is a dream, and prior to this dream, you must be sleeping. Sleeping is ignorance. When you wake up from this state, you wake up to awareness.

Since being around you, I don't quite know if I am awake or not, anymore.

No knowing is good. For knowing, you need someone else to know about you, or to be known by you. Here you are alone. This is the ultimate truth.

Nothing ever appeared and nothing will ever disappear. You are alone. That is all. And this aloneness is beyond where the sun can shine or enlighten.

***

In all languages except Sanskrit, self refers to ego or some personalized individuality. In Sanskrit, Self is defined as Brahman, which has no other meaning but Brahman. Brahman itself is That itself.

You are not to ask for any clarification. It is not graspable. Not by the senses or the mind. It is untouched and unspoken. This is It, itself. Therefore leave it alone.

Brahman is all. It cannot be defined. Everything. Eternal. That in which the cosmos is dwelling, in which all of us are dwelling. It is that Brahman which dwells in all hearts. In the hearts of all beings: humans, animals, birds, marine life, and rocks. This Brahman dwells in each heart. And all dwell in Brahman.

***

Somehow we imagine that we are separate from Brahman, as the wave imagines itself separate from the ocean. "How? Why?" Let it alone. Let us not speak about it.

When you are sitting under a tree resting, and a snake falls from the tree onto your shoulder, will you look at the tree from where it has fallen? Or do you wonder about what kind of snake this is? If you do, it will be too late for this analysis. Better to throw it away as soon as it falls.

Somehow we are separated from our own Self. And very few of us among the six billion humans—let alone all the other species, so many we cannot count—very few are here with the sole desire to return home.

So, what is the quickest way possible, so as not to waste any time? Many of you have told me that you have spent ten, twelve, twenty years with many teachers.

You have searched for peace, freedom, enlightenment. And nothing has happened. You say, "I am still not free. I have read the books, done all kinds of therapies, meditations, and yogas. Nothing has happened. I am still not finished."

Here, no method, way, or therapy is taught. There are no books to be dealt with. The real aim has nothing to do with the study of books. What is missing in books is experience. No book can give you experience by studying it. You are here to experience directly.

You may read the menu for a number of years—staying in the restaurant from morning to evening reading the menu. Talking to the receptionist or making friends with the waiters is not the way. The way is to order your food straightaway and eat it. Eat it and that's all. You need not go to another restaurant, because you have done it. You have had the direct experience.

When you eat, you appease the hunger which brought you to the restaurant. If you go to a restaurant and only read the menu, your hunger will not be satisfied. If the restaurant offers clay display dishes, you cannot eat them. If you do eat the display dishes, you will not be satisfied.

***

My dear friends, you are here. I am happy. I am very happy with the results also. I am very much encouraged. Some people are giving me absolute joy. But I am requesting every one of you who are here—there are quite enough of you right here for the whole world—to give light to everybody. Only one matchstick can burn a whole forest of ignorance. Just try one match, "I am free," and ignorance is burned instantly.

MEDITATION

Any practice, anything that involves time, cannot take you out of bondage. Anything done with the concept of time cannot lead you to freedom beyond time. You have to jump out of time. What is time except "I am the body"? Can you conceive of time without the concept "I am the body"? To think "I am so-and-so, and I want this or that" is arrogance.

***

To break your habit of running out through the senses, to control the mind, meditation is absolutely necessary. The outgoing habit of the mind can be arrested in meditation. It has to be effortless meditation, not yogic.

While yogic meditation may give you more consciousness of the body, I am speaking here of meditation for freedom, which is observing the mind at its source. Calmness can be attained from yogic meditation, but when the meditation is over, the habit of mind remains. This is because it is body-oriented, not freedom-oriented.

For freedom, which needs no time, meditation is inquiry into the Self. All the outward tendencies of mind are arrested. Just observe the source of *I*. Observe where the thought arises from. Vigilant! Alert! Effortless! Find out. When the *I* arises, body and manifestation arise. This manifestation is your projection based on your notion of *I am*.

***

I have so many concepts about exercises I've read in books.

Many methods are prescribed for different temperaments. All methods teach you to do something. It may be physical, oral, or mental activity. All these exercises involve mental gymnastics. You never keep quiet. Nobody teaches this simple truth.

If you are quiet, the religions will fail. The false teachings will fail. Just keep quiet. That is the way to find peace and love among people. Keep quiet. Then the whole structure of religion will collapse. Religions give you fear: fear of hell. If you don't do this, you will go to hell. All religions preach this fear. All religions are based on the fear of hell. No religion teaches you to just keep quiet.

If you keep quiet, for just a few minutes out of your entire span of life, perhaps you will win peace. That's the way to approach reality, liberation, nirvana. Keep quiet.

This is up to you. According to their temperaments, people select their own way and follow their own way. Very few will keep quiet for even five minutes. Instead, they go to the Himalayas; they go to the temples; they go on pilgrimages. But very few just spend five minutes in their house keeping quiet.

Then there is no need for a teacher. If the teacher says, "Just keep quiet," then the business of the teacher doesn't flourish.

If the teacher says, "You've got nothing to do whatsoever; you are just to keep quiet," why is the teacher needed? His business will not run, so he has to tell you to do something. No religion will be confirmed. No books will be published. No teaching will flourish. Just to be quiet. And without quiet, there is no rest anywhere.

***

In the past I have memories of bliss and pleasure, and when I am sitting I always expect it should be like this. I don't want only quiet. I expect it has to be something more.

I say, don't expect anything! Your mind has projected a manifestation, and then it runs after the projection. It will not give you peace. So find out from where this expectation arises. You have not fulfilled this expectation in any other way. Now you can spend a few minutes discovering where this expectation arises from.

Instead of running out with the senses, the mind is arrested and directed to its source. What you want is peace of mind, right?

Yes.

So now you can help yourself. You have gone to so many gurus and ashrams; have you benefited?

I can do exercises that benefit me sometimes.

Exercises are no problem. You can't sit all the time. Some yoga maintains the body, and this is no problem. If your body is sick, you can do certain things to maintain your body: some physical exercise, good sattvic food, or simple yoga.

However, if you are using exercise for some gain, this is something else. All search for powers is done with ego, with the thought "I am doing."

I once met a man in the Himalayas who had many powers. He could levitate [sit in the air]. He had the powers of manifestation. But his guru said at the time of his death, "I have shown you everything I know, but I did not find the ultimate truth. So seek someone who can give you ultimate truth."

If you don't desire anything, all that exists is given unto you, unasked for. Does the king say, "I want this building or that building"? The whole kingdom is his. It will be given unto you. You won't have to beg anymore anywhere.

***

There are so many practices or exercises or sadhanas being practiced around the world. Forms of yoga, mantra, worship, karma, devotion, and so on.

The question is: What is the goal? What do you want? Different practices are for different aims or goals. Perhaps we can speak of Brahman, because you may believe that *I* means individual consciousness. Here, Brahman is that which is without any attributes. A mass of knowledge itself, which is association-less. No duality whatsoever. This is called Brahman.

Here, the goal is attributeless Brahman, beyond the reach of mind or intellect. It reveals itself by itself, because it is beyond mind or intellect or senses or any kind of practice. It is self-revealing. To find something in the darkness, you need light. To see the light, you don't need a light. It is the light itself. Self-revealing. Self-luminous. No association is possible because it is attributeless.

What is being advised here is to realize the attributeless, immaculate, eternal Brahman. Practices may be purifying, or may give some temporary relief. What kind of exercise is nearest to your goal?

The few people who want to realize absolute Brahman meditate on the attributeless Brahman alone. No object of concentration is possible with attributeless Brahman. No focus on an object of the past, present, or future. Meditate on immaculate Brahman, which is not other than your own Atman, your own fundamental nature.

If you are not able to immediately follow what is happening here, you can continue this practice for a while. Slowly you will see that the meditator and the meditated-upon vanish.

If you want to think something, why think "I am the body" or something which is not lasting? If you want to have a thought, and you cannot be without a thought, why not think "I am Brahman"? If you want practice, then "I am Brahman" would be the nearest practice. This exercise is nearest to your goal.

Every ashram, every center, will give you some therapy or practice to keep you busy. Why? Because no one there has realized the truth to say, "Just keep quiet."

If they tell you to just keep quiet, what is the purpose of the center or ashram? Its commercial purpose will fail. What could be a better teacher or a better teaching than "Keep quiet"? This is the teaching of my master.

In this century, who else has given this teaching? He is the only teacher of this century who could say, "Keep quiet." To keep quiet is the only way to do away with this cycle of suffering.

Practices, rituals, mantras, or doing yoga are very good, because something in this direction is better than getting lost in the world. Some of you have already directly experienced the truth; others want further clarification; some do not understand what is happening here. Let me explain. Whatever practice you do focuses on a particular center. Physical practice is the body. Vital practices are pranayama, kundalini, kriya, and so forth. Raja yoga and intellectual practices focus on the mental center.

As your nature is always consciousness, never is there a time when consciousness is not present. When you are in the waking state and active in worldly or spiritual activities, you are very conscious of what you are doing. Even in the dream state you are conscious of dreamer and dream. Sometimes you are brought back to your next waking state, and you are conscious of what was dreamt about. You are also conscious of the joy you have experienced during sleep with no dreams.

By rejecting the other states of waking, dreaming, and sleeping, the mind is at rest, at peace. And in this peace you are very conscious!

This consciousness is present in all states. Consciousness is the basis, the fountain, the source. No word can describe what it is. But neither can you deny that consciousness is ever-existent. Consciousness is existence itself! Bliss itself! This cannot be denied.

Seeing the maturity of people here now in satsang, we can speak of these things and they can get it. Some of you experience this, and you report your experience. I am very happy about it.

I don't experience the world that way. It seems there are times when I am not sure I am conscious.

You deny consciousness, right?

Right.

Are you not conscious of the denial? Like this. [*laughter*]

***

In my Buddhist meditation practice for twenty years, I have been investigating myself.

This is investigation which is going on right now, and you are running away. Investigate. Go in!

What have you been doing for these twenty years?

I've been looking in, and I have seen emptiness of self and phenomena. I feel like I have gained a lot. Not *I*, but I feel like understanding has arisen.

That understanding was borrowed. That word "emptiness" you are using, which is full of egoism, is not emptiness. Just a borrowed concept. This emptiness of which we are speaking is not emptiness. Not even emptiness. Emptiness has nothing to do with it. Let go of this word "emptiness."

Where did you learn it? You heard it somewhere. It belongs to the past. It has nothing to do with what we are speaking of.

The word "emptiness" is just pointing to something else, like the finger pointing to the moon. You must reject the finger to see the moon. Reject the word "emptiness" if you want to go beyond. It is a finger pointing to something that I don't give any name.

So I wasted those twenty years, hmmm?

Those twenty years brought you here. Not only twenty years—thirty-five million years.

But, in truth, there is no time; nothing ever existed at all. This is the experience; this is the ultimate experience. Time appears in the fraud of the mind. You touch the word "I" and simultaneously time will arise: past, present, and future. This truth is unspeakable. The Buddha spoke for forty-nine years, and still, I don't think he ever touched the point of the unspeakable.

***

When I meditate, I feel the need for contact with people. What should I do?

When you meditate, meditate. When you are with people, be with people.

No. When I meditate I can't, because I am afraid of being alone.

This aloneness is the start of meditation. Before aloneness there is no meditation, because then you are with something else. When there is nothing else, then your meditation begins.

For fear to be there, there must be an idea of another. With another comes fear, not before. There may be fear before you begin meditation—fear of leaving everything behind, or fear of the unknown in front of you. You have not yet entered meditation at this point.

Meditation is love with your own Self. Not anybody else.

What is meditation?

Meditation is concentrating on the awareness itself which has always been there. Are you not aware when you meditate? If you are in your psyche, you must be aware. Being aware of this awareness is called meditation. And that awareness will reveal the truth to you.

You keep aware, and awareness will reveal the truth of itself. This is called meditation. What fear can there be? Awareness is meditating on truth. Awareness meditating on itself is meditation, not on some object.

***

When meditating, thoughts come to trouble me. What should I do?

Suppose you are meditating now. Pick up a thought and tell me.

I have an image.

Image is a thought itself. What were you thinking?

I was thinking about my master.

Continue thinking about your master. Now let this thought be replaced by another thought. Look at the next thought that has taken its place.

I thought about my parents.

Good. Now, what did you do with the thought of the master?

Still somewhere in my mind.

No, not somewhere. Mind is thought. No difference. When the master thought goes away, now there is the thought of your parents. Now hold this thought of parents. Hold firmly. Look for another, more important thought, a superior thought. Master is gone. Good. Now remove parents, and what is there?

My sister.

Okay, hold on to this sister thought tightly and tell me the next thought.

My sister's children.

Okay, look. Master you have rejected. Let him go to hell; it doesn't matter. Next, parents—rejected. You always keep in mind the best, that which you love the most. The parents have replaced the master. They are dearer than the master.

When you marry you forget your parents. You forget everything for love of your husband. You can only have one thing in your mind at a time. Always our thoughts are of what we hold dear.

How did you lose this thought of the master? The master must be the one who gives you peace of mind, gives you liberation from bondage, who relieves you of suffering. If you give it up for parents, and then sister and then children, this is disturbance of mind.

First of all, you must have passed through millions of species to be a human being. We have a choice that perhaps other species don't have. This is a choice to be made or rejected. This is the choice you made when you went to your master. You went to a master for freedom. How can you reject this for parents and sister?

I didn't go to the master for freedom.

For what then, music? If you did not go for freedom, that is why you rejected the master.

What do you mean by "master," and what is your desire then?

I want enlightenment. I want to be closer to God.

If you are close to God, this is called freedom from suffering, freedom from the world process. You went to the master to teach you how to be closer to God, didn't you?

Yes.

Now, a very good thought. With this thought, reject all other thoughts, all other relations. You come to a teacher to be told how to get close to God. Now you have found the teacher who will introduce you to God. Instead of holding on to this thought, this thought of the master which enables you to get close to God, you replaced it with a superior one.

Superior?

Of course. It can only be replaced this way. You choose to think about the superior, more desirable thing.

There is no other superior thought.

Hold on to this thought then. Now, while holding this thought, look for another to replace it. Be careful. This is a very important thought. That is why you came here. If you replace it, you go from God.

Either you stay here, or you get out of it. There is no other option now. So choose.

I cannot think of another thought.

Very nice. You can't. Now, don't let go of this thought if there is nothing superior to this. If you miss this chance, you will have missed it, the most important thought in this human life. A blessed person to give rise to this thought. No other thoughts can touch you.

[*long silence*] Okay, ten minutes have passed. Have you found another, more important thought to replace this one?

No.

Unless you give up this thought, you cannot catch another thought. Nothing can touch the true thought, "I want to be free." Otherwise, you bring in your parents. Even cows have parents, and sisters and children.

So how to be successful? If you want to study medicine, do you go to the gambling den? Can you become a doctor this way? Look carefully at what you want, and stay there.

I rejected my parents. I rejected my family. I went to my master. Nothing could improve this thought, "I want to be free." Nothing could take me away from the master. Twenty-four hours a day, this thought of God was in my head.

***

To find permanent joy, you must look in the right direction. You will not find it in any outside object. Every object will rise, stay, and then cease. You have to look somewhere else for permanent, eternal joy. Don't attribute joy to something else, be it a person, the sun, moon, or stars.

Stop this tendency of going to outside objects, whatever they may be. Stop your mind from going in any direction outside. Then you must return to your inner beauty. That is your own nature: bliss eternal, which you have never felt.

You may be having pleasure, you may be having beautiful sights outside, but I don't think anybody has been satisfied by clinging to any outside beauty or outside happiness.

So don't waste your life with externalities. Check your mind and keep it from this outward tendency which has been going on for millions of years.

And now is the time. You are here. You must stop all the past tendencies of the mind to flow outward. Then redirect the mind to your own Self. There must be Self that is attributing beauty to the sun, stars, and rest of world. So find out who this Self is that is the endless reservoir of beauty, love, and happiness that you have missed all along.

The mind is always running after momentary pleasures, and jumping to the next one, endlessly. If you want to end this affair once and for all, then stop it and direct it to its own source. Then you will know the beauty of this reservoir. Then your mind will be submerged in it and dissolve once and for all.

This mind is so treacherous, and you have also given a long rope to it. Therefore, it is not its fault. One day you have to decide, and this is the time. You are here for satsang. This is satsang. And you have to find eternal peace. There is not much strenuous practice for this. It has to be what is already here waiting for you in this very moment. This moment is quite enough.

***

I was here for three weeks, and you cut me free from my arrogance of misery. Then I went to Poona and, for five weeks, I did tantra. Now I am confused. Because I got very much into anger, hurt, jealousy, rage, attached to expectations with a friend that didn't happen the way I wanted it to happen. Now I feel shaky.

So? What do you want?

What to do when the emotions come? Part of me wants to fight. How to stop them? Just inquire "Who am I?"

How to stop? To stop it, you have come here. There is no therapy here. Anyone who says "do this" or "do that" is a butcher, not a guide. No true teacher says "do this" or "do that." Understand?

The person who tells you, "Enough! You have done enough. Now keep quiet"—he is the person to stay with for a while. Otherwise, everybody is involved in therapies and that is your karma.

Why don't you keep quiet? Therapy is with mind, isn't it? Body, feelings, and mind. Can you do any therapy without mind and without the body?

Here you need neither. Don't use your mind or your body for one minute, and you experience eternal peace. Stay quiet for an instant and you will know what arises, what comes.

***

I seem to experience more Being with eyes closed. I wonder about techniques of meditation that are taught.

You speak of Being and you speak of techniques. One is swimming in the river, and the other is staying in your room with a book in hand that teaches you how to swim. Lying in your bed, reading about how to dive into the river—this is a technique of Being.

Yes, but there are different ways of going into the river: head first or feet first or plunging into it.

Plunging is what I say. Plunging is addressing yourself directly. Throw away your book! In the river, you don't need this book to read. If you have to learn swimming, enter into the river. Don't lie on your bed. You have not met the river. If you have not come to the river, technique will not make you a swimmer. Enter into the river. Enter into Being itself and give up all techniques.

But it seems to matter if my eyes are open or closed.

Does it matter to the sun if the shades are open? Blind people can have their eyes closed all the time. Are they looking within? Eyes have nothing to do with it. Eyes are for seeing, not for Being. No eyes, ears, nose, tongue, or touch are needed. You are already That.

The mind has taken you out through these windows. But if you are That itself, then you do not care if the windows are open or closed. Remove the dust from your eyes; then open or closed does not matter. But first remove the dust. What is this dust of the eyes that does not see Being? This dust is thought. Let no thought arise. If it arises, there is dust in the eyes, the ears, and the nose. You don't hear the music; you don't smell perfume. You don't see your own light within.

And if you don't see your own light, you will see other things: reflections. If you don't hear your own music, you are attracted only to outside noises. Why don't you smell your own perfume? Have you smelled the perfume of your own lotus? If you stop smelling the garbage of thought, you will be attracted to your own thousand-petaled lotus. It is within everyone.

When you see your own Being, you know beauty, love, immaculate eternity.

You will not leave it. You will not leave Being.

Thought takes you to becoming: I am this or that. If you get rid of all this dust, your eyes will be very clear. There will be no inside or outside. Your ears will hear music.

Your mind will be as beautiful as the most intimate friend. It will take you to where it comes from, introducing you to that glory. You must make use of your mind, as far as possible.

But pure mind, not dusty mind. Dusty mind is desires. Keep desires out, and there is no difference between mind, Atman, Self, or consciousness. Then mind is no-mind.

Only desire pollutes the mind. Abandon desire and see what it is, for a few instants. Undress yourself of all desires and plunge into the eternal Ganga. Take a bath of purity, completely naked of all desires, and then come out, put on your dress, and move freely in this manifestation. Do as you like. No pressure. You have to choose what you want: happiness or suffering. Choose. Eternity or destruction, hatred or love—choose, okay?

***

Is freedom from thought really freedom from ego?

Yes! Ego doesn't exist. It's just a concept that you hear from somewhere else. When a child is born he has no ego. He's very happy, smiling at everybody. Ego is a past concept.

In no-thought, is not ego latent? In a moment of no-thought, bliss comes—then again the ego arises, so the ego is latent.

In this particular case, when you entered into this thoughtless state—from ego to egoless state—you made an effort. To arrive into egolessness, to Self, to light, you have fastened yourself with a rope, with the ego, by making an effort. This rope, the ego, will pull you back.

Now, don't tie. No effort and no rope. Then enter into this effortlessness. It is already there! There is no entrance, and no exit either! Exit and entrance are the past and future. So I say, break the link with this past and future. And how will you come out? Everything is truth. Who will call you back?

There is no ego. Ego has been dumped on you by someone else. Your parents, society, the church. That's all. There is no ego. Egolessness, freedom, is your birthright. It is your inheritance of happiness. That is why you seek it. Everything that you do, you do for happiness, peace of mind, and love.

Where did you get this concept, first of all? You have tasted happiness once, and so you want it again. But you are searching in places where happiness is not: in objects, in sense pleasures.

I do yoga and breath control with my meditation to reach emptiness, but I always return.

If someone enters into meditation, he first ties a rope: "I will sit in meditation for one hour and then I have to go to the office." This man is looking at the time. Meditation is dhyana, and dhyana is when the mind is no-mind. This is meditation. When you meditate, there should be no meditator and no meditated-upon. This is meditation.

But there is no consciousness of body then.

There is no ego then. This is your nature. Everything is there, all the cosmos is there, and you are perfect. You don't need anything. It is limitless. You can't cross any frontier into another country. Wherever you go, front is emptiness; back is emptiness; sides are emptiness. This is wisdom.

If the rope is tied by ego and I admit, "Yes, the rope is tied," is not some effort needed to untie the rope? If I sit and do nothing—

Even sitting is making an effort. Standing is making an effort.

So some effort is always there.

Some effort is always there, and when you don't connect with these so-called efforts, don't cling, you will arrive somewhere that is revealed by effortlessness. Efforts are all precepts and concepts.

***

Can anyone benefit from sadhanas?

Sadhana is not for freedom, but to remove your old habits. Freedom is standing in front of you, smiling at you, as you do your sadhana. Your old tendencies, which you grasp, are an imaginary wall. This wall is the thought "I am bound and suffering."

***

Everyone I know is engaged in some sort of spiritual practice, whether Vipassana or Zen or psychotherapy, to get closer to waking up. Does it have any value?

No value. They are wasting time because they have nothing else to do. They have entered into a trade to cheat themselves.

But so many religions, so many teachings and practices, so many paths—

All destructive. What is the result? With religion, what is the first result? Destruction on the basis of religion. So far, the number of people killed is equal to the world population, and it is still going on. And who is the one who is enlightened through any practice? That, I want to know!

Well, it's rare—

Tell me anyone. Since you have asked the question, you tell me: Is there anyone who has been freed through practice?

I know a handful of people who have received some level of awakening.

Anyone. You name anyone from the beginning of this planet.

Buddha.

Yes. He went from teacher to teacher and was not satisfied. He went to many sects and teachers and said, "This is not it, so I will do it myself."

Then he sat by himself. He sat in meditation by himself under the bodhi tree. Something happened.

No one knows what. Ananda was the first person who went near him. "Master, what has happened? What have you experienced, what do you feel?"

If he got something, it could have been that he left everything to get freedom. Freedom cannot be the result of any effort, because then freedom would be dependent on something else, and that is not truth. Truth is self-shining and self-effulgent. It does not need any other help to be known. The diamond does not need something else to be a diamond. Only when you reject this effort can something happen.

Yes, but a diamond is rough and needs to be worked to be cut and made beautiful. Spiritual practice could be said to take the rough human being and refine it so that the shining light will come through. The Buddha meditated, so people sit to become enlightened.

He realized himself. The realization is that freedom is already here. If he did any practice, it was to ward off this concept of effort, that effort is needed for freedom. When that goes, freedom is here.

Osho said that he practiced and practiced and then let go. There was no effort.

Practice is to remove the habit of practice. Then realize that freedom is already here. What is here right now needs no practice. Just see what the impediments are. What is the wall? The wall is imagining that you are not free. When you make an effort to be free, you accept the concept that you are not free, so you start from there. If you get rid of this concept that "I am not free," what will happen? This imagination is your own creation.

Even this intention, "I want to be free"—from where does it arise? Don't do anything; just see where the intention is arising from. Is it coming from where the intention is trying to take you? Even "I am bound"—where does it arise from?

From consciousness.

Yes, okay. Very good. From consciousness. So now the idea "I want to be free" arises, and someone suggests some practice. If successful, where will that practice take you? What is the end of that practice?

Freedom.

So what is the difference between pre-effort consciousness and post-practice freedom?

Same.

So the distance between two samenesses—how far do you have to travel?

Practice to return to the same place.

So, if you know it earlier?

THE NATURE OF MIND AND VASANAS

Consciousness alone is. When it tries to understand itself, this understanding has become mind. There is no difference between understanding and mind. Mind means activity. Whatever your mind is, so will be your activity. As your understanding is, so is your mind. As your mind, so your activity.

This activity creates the five senses. Respective objects are created, and this is called the universe. This universe is the result of understanding, which once arose to understand consciousness. Consciousness, which cannot be objectified, is made an object. The mind becomes the subject to perceive the objects.

Whatever we see, whatever we understand, is nothing but ignorance. This is because when this understanding arises, it creates mind, and the mind becomes *I am.I am* needs to understand something and act. This activity from *I am* is misunderstanding, because consciousness cannot be understood, perceived, or conceived. It has no other observer. It is self-effulgent, omnipresent, omniscient. Who could be its observer?

Understanding has objectified it, and it has become subjective self. Being subject, it needs to create. This creation is the result of ignorance. In this ignorance, whatever you understand, conceive, or perceive is just ignorance.

The creation vanishes in an instant, just as it arises. *I* is the mind, and objects are the universe. Utter "I" and there is the universe—past, present, future—and endless repetition. This is samsara.

You misconceived a snake in the rope. When you have knowledge of the rope, the snake disappears. Why? Because it was a misunderstanding that it was a snake. This knowledge of the rope will instantly be responsible for the disappearance of the snake.

From the beginning, the first ignorance is the arising of *I am.* Return back from samsara; turn away from the objects, activities, mind, and senses.

Return to the *I,* the first activity of understanding.

Consciousness itself wanted to understand, and arose like a wave in the ocean. This wave, this samsara, ceases when we stop this understanding. With this decision to stop, do away with this first understanding from where *I am* arises, which is mind, ego, objects, and samsara.

Just don't understand anything. How? Keep quiet. Keep quiet means no activity. It is your nature. This way is no way! Activity comes from disturbance of mind. When the mind is not disturbed, the ocean is not agitated. There is no wave. Consciousness is consciousness alone. It is absolute, perfect limitlessness. Immaculate fathomlessness. You can't understand it or describe it. This is consciousness, existence, bliss.

It is already here. What is seen is the result of this light, this beauty. The sun is shining because of this light. If there is one candle, and a hundred candles are kindled from it, the candles can be different but the flame remains the same.

How does the flame of the first candle differ from the last? Unfortunately, most don't look at the flame; instead, they count the candles. You see so many individual things. You do not see the flame.

Consciousness is the original flame. With consciousness you see everything, like in a mirror. A very small mirror can reflect the mountains, the forests, and the sky. If you look at this mirror which is inside you, you can see anything.

All that you see is your projection as the dreamer. Whenever you see anything, you are dreaming! When you don't see anything, you are awake.

Multiplicity is a dream. You can instantly wake up. How? Don't agitate your mind. Don't give rise to the wave *I am.* As it rises, so it can vanish.

You are now so attached to this long-standing dream. That is why there is suffering and tension. Some here and there will decide, "Enough!" From here, a desire will arise, "I want to be free." This desire is not different from consciousness or freedom itself. *I am* dissolves back into freedom, from where it arose.

**

The trance of the mind starts with an unarisen thought. This thought then arises. Unarisen has to arise. What the wave was before was unarisen in the ocean.

So look at the unarisen wave. Waveless space. Look, before it arises, and nip the bud itself. I am asking you to not allow the wave to arise. Before the rise of the wave, it is unarisen thought. Thought has to arise, then arising, then trouble, right? It goes, and then another one comes. Unarisen, arising, and then falling. This is the process of life. Realizing this is checking the trance of the mind.

Right now, simply invite an unarisen thought. This is to see the den of the bandits, from where they will come to steal and break into your house. Bring up a thought now; invite an unarisen thought to come. [*silence*] Now invite a thought. Have a thought come. This is checking the train of the mind. This is vigilance. This is watchfulness. This must be your habit! And this is a natural habit. It is natural happiness also. It doesn't cost you anything.

If you allow a thought to arise, you are in trouble. Then there is this cycle of endless troubles. If you are not vigilant it will arise, and this rise is called samsara. Understand?

And if you look for it? Nirvana. Simple. Look for it, and where is samsara? [*laughs*] If you know this, where is samsara? If you don't, endless samsara.

When you want to get rid of it, you want freedom. Do it. There is some secret in this. If you do it, you will get it. And when you get it, then we will tell each other. Otherwise, if I tell you before you discover it yourself, you may not agree.

Do it first, and tell me the secret. Keep digging into unarisen thought and see what happens.

I am at the thieves' den. It is all light and activity.

Yes, okay. Go further then. Keep going further in. It is a very beautiful dance, really. It is a romance. I speak about bliss. Everything combined together—existence, knowledge, bliss, consciousness—together dancing. You simply do this and look around.

The den became a wave.

Very good, very good. Still beyond. Still beyond.

There is nothing there!

That's it. Now you've got it. Stay here.

***

I feel so unworthy, like a liar, because I've had so many experiences, but still the mind returns.

Have you seen the mind, really? It's a ghost. It doesn't really exist. As soon as you desire something, this ghost of a mind arises. If you desire anything, then this ghost of the mind will trouble you. Get rid of desire, and where is the mind?

Where there is desire, there is trouble. You can live very well without the mind. Without the mind, you are wise; with the mind, you are stupid. Desire nothing and you are emperor of this kingdom. You are peace, beauty, and love. Reject the mind for some time and see.

In the evening you go on the road; you see a snake and you are afraid. You pick up a stick and you beat it. It doesn't move and you see it is a rope. Fear is gone and you throw away the stick.

If you address the mind with "Who are you?" it will disappear. Look at the snake of the mind and discover if it is real. Thoughts are impediments to seeing your own face. Don't give rise to any thought, and discover who you are.

***

For the last few days I have been having a recurring dream of falling. Falling from a great height, falling in the ocean, and I wake up with fear. Is this connected with what's going on here?

These are dormant vasanas—desires and tendencies in the unconscious mind. Meditation or understanding or inquiry is stirring them up. There is mud on the bottom, yet it appears clear. When you stir it, what will happen? This inquiry is to stir things up. When stirred, it will come up; then it disappears.

You now know what you did not know was there. When you meditate, the dormant dirt that was lying in the unconscious mind gets stirred up. You have never been aware of it before. It was lying in wait, to later become your next incarnation, slowly, when the time comes.

Now it is disturbed with meditation, with quietness of mind. It is disturbed. It comes up. What comes up disappears. You can see the dirt now. Throw out the dirt.

Otherwise, carry on as everyone else does. Nobody cares. This is called the cycle of birth and death. If you don't stir these dormant tendencies, you will let them settle to the bottom. Then you go on accumulating fresh desires, and you go on and on accumulating. This cycle will be endless.

In the next life, the desires from the bottom will be the first to appear. Then new ones will settle to the bottom. This is the circle of birth and death.

You must inquire, "Who am I?" This inquiry will consume everything, burn everything, which is lying in the path of it.

The future will not come because of the purity of the mind. In the future, the bottom is not dirty. Everything has been stirred up and burned. Present will stay. In the present, you are not the doer when you know who you are. Therefore, the activity of action will leave no footprints. Therefore, no link with past or future; and in between, what do you see?

Now.

Yes. The mind takes you always to the past—past pleasures and habits. Then you are chewing the old habits. Fresh is only to find out your true face now. This is the courage. If you stay here, you have crossed the ocean. Your work is done.

***

This last week has been very hard. I've been tested, and it is not easy.

Yes, very good. For millions of years you have been asleep and you have been robbed. You did not complain then that it was hard. Just like a drunk lying in the gutter does not complain. But when you are surrounded by purity, you notice the single stain and you don't like it. A drunk lies anywhere and doesn't care.

Everything buried dormant in the mind is coming up. This satsang is stirring it up. All the tendencies will come up to leave you. Otherwise, you are only adding dust to dust. Picking up desires endlessly.

Now you have put an end to desire. The accumulated storehouse has to rise up when circumstances allow. Tendencies have to rise up to leave because you are not giving them a chance to play. You are already engaged somewhere else. This is the "hard time" you speak of.

If you don't aspire to freedom, it won't be a hard time. You will live like nearly six billion people live. One man chose a hard life. He was a prince 2,535 years ago. Which truly served him: the hard life or the easy life? He walked away from the easy life. He turned his back on his family and his kingdom and headed toward the hard life. He took a begging bowl in hand, took off the king's robe, and opted for the hard life. Out of billions, he is still being remembered. And you are complaining after one week!

Face toward the Self, the Atman, and you are safe. Look back, and you are gone. Face toward the Self, and who can break you? Twenty-four hours, incessantly. If you are in love, it has to be twenty-four hours. You don't say, "For twenty-three hours, I will love you, and for one hour, I will slip out to the red-light district."

You must have turned your back and gone somewhere else when you speak of a hard time. This is your home. How can it be a hard time at home? Who is not happy at home?

***

We were speaking about ecstasy, peace, love, and happiness. Nowhere on the face of the earth do you find it. You can go on pilgrimages, go to churches, valleys, or mountains. Even gods are not having peace. They are searching in the wrong place. They are searching in cement bricks! Any direction that you go, you will not see peace or happiness or love anywhere.

Stop all that! Don't waste time! Stay where you are! This is the dharma that will help you. All else is adharma—senses and bodies.

Stay where you are and find out, where is the peace? Nearest of all. Nearer than your own retina. The mind has been cheating you for thirty-five million years, my dear children. You have been cheated. Stop this, now! Look here and know who you are. Instantly you will find freedom, and this suffering—hitchhiking from womb to womb—will instantly stop. The only way is to look within.

Experiences have been experienced, and they have not given you peace. Wherever there is no experiencer, there is no experience. So disappear! Experienced, experience, experiencer—let them all disappear right now.

You proceed toward that which is unknown by the senses. Now you have to cheat the mind itself, which has been deceiving you all these years. This is your time now.

Question the mind: "Who are you? You have been deceiving me. Now I have seen this thief through eyes, ears, nose, tongue, and touch. Now I have seen who this troublemaker was. Now I am not going to listen to you. I will do it myself."

Break off relations with the mind itself. Then you are left alone. Your mind has been troubling you. Your priests have been troubling you. Your church and your society have been troubling you. Your country has been troubling you. Mind you, enough! Stay by yourself, and find out now. Look around. For some time, don't touch anybody or anything that you have known, seen, heard, or touched.

Most of the religions are cheating you. Most of the religions are cheating the poor people. "Do this and I will send you to heaven." Don't listen to any of these people. Find out, where is heaven? Heaven will come down to you.

Stay alone. Don't allow yourself to be touched by anybody. If you get rid of this mind, mind will leave you. Your cravings will leave; your notions will leave; your desires will leave; your ideations will leave. Everything is going to leave.

Now what will happen? If all the known is rejected, in front of you is the unknown. If you have given up the cravings and desires for the known, what is left is unknown. You have become unknown and merge into the unknown, because they are identical.

Your identity with the known has been troubling you thus far: "This is me and this is mine." Perhaps from the unknown you will enter into emptiness, and from this emptiness you will see that all this projection is your playground.

You will not have any hate toward anybody. This is the region of love. You will see previously known people, and now you will love them. You will love their Selves and they will love you. This is the trick of life. You will enjoy this life. This planet will become heaven. Whatever you see, you will see beauty. Whatever you hear, you will hear the music of your own Self, your own inner light. Whatever you speak, you will speak sutras, wisdom. This has to happen this very instant. Don't have any doubt. Doubt hasn't helped you.

This is the romance with your own Self. Nobody to cheat or depend upon. Hitherto, you have been loving perishable things. Everybody is perishable and facing death. How can you love a corpse? How can you love what is not eternal, not permanent, not love, and not everlasting, abiding, eternity itself?

Find out who your friend is. Who is more intimate than eternity? If you want to love, make love with eternity. It is your own nature. It is your own mother. Otherwise, forgetting her, you go with others. You go for kicks somewhere else.

Therefore, stop, for one instant. Everything will be given to you. If you return back to your country, it is your responsibility to help everybody. Once you get something, you know you have love; you have seen truth face-to-face. Be a representative of truth. Not man to man. Truth only will serve people. Go door to door and give them love. Tell them that you are happy, at peace, in love. They are all your relations, your own Self.

Not only human beings. You will see the same life in animals, in trees, the same life in rocks. You can even speak to rocks. Wherever you look, look with love, and you will get a response from rocks, from trees, from animals, from human beings.

First you dissolve yourself into reality, into truth. Then it will be so attractive, and everyone will be attracted to you. You will be so beautiful because you will not be claiming anything. Beauty does not desire anything. Inner light will shine, and this will do the work. It is not you who are doing, nor is it someone else.

Inner light, inner wisdom, is guiding you. You don't see it, so you don't believe it. When anything good or big happens, you say, "I have done it!" And when it goes bad, you blame God. This is arrogance.

This is a very simple affair. Don't postpone it. You can do it here, now.

***

Something I don't understand: Usually, in my life, I have a lot of energy to create things and do things.

Now this is the second time I've come here.

It's like I've taken a drug—it's nice, but the whole day I'm finished. Is all my energy and creativity just mind?

Yes! [*enormous laughter*]

But I can't just lie in bed all day.

It's your energy that brings you here, and when you get here, this same energy is quiet.

But how am I going to do anything?

You will do wonderfully well by not doing! You simply stay quiet. Something else is going to take charge of you. You simply watch what happens, and you keep quiet.

You don't keep quiet; therefore, you are in trouble. Just keep quiet, and let something arise from within: that peace you have never seen before. Keep quiet for some time, and it will reveal itself. This is my advice.

***

In the Gita, Krishna says that, in order to move, some effort is there—even to eat.

It is not generally understood what Krishna meant. Eating needs effort;

seeing needs effort. But it is Krishna who is speaking. It is through Krishna that all effort is made. You are eating; hands are moving; tongue is moving; munching is going on; digestion is going on. What is the power through which the hand moves, the mouth chews, and so on?

I see. So Krishna does all that. So I should untie the rope and let Krishna do the—

Even Krishna is a rope! [*laughter*]

Any name and any form is a rope. What is that which is not a rope? It must be your own consciousness. You don't need these ropes, and Krishna knew it very well.

Krishna means "untouched." Everybody is untouched. You have a dream, and in the dream you fall in love with a girl. You're celebrating your wedding and calling friends, and then you awake. You are untouched. Nothing to do with those festivities. All that was a dream.

Therefore, wake up, wake up! Your house is on fire from all directions. Don't sleep! Wake up!

What is waking up? Establishment firmly into the Self, by the Self, with the Self, for the Self. Self is untouched. Absolutely untouched. This manifestation is your Leela—this Brahma, Vishnu, Mahesh [Shiva] is your Leela.

Unless you wake up, you will carry unfulfilled desires along with you. Unless you wake up, you will carry these bundles, this baggage of unfulfilled desires, and to fulfill these, you will again select a womb.

So what to do about unfulfilled desires? Some teachers suggest you have them fulfilled. So you pick up one desire to fulfill, and out of the relationship of fulfilling this desire, there will be hundreds of other desires. They will also stand in the queue!

When you have any relation or connection with any desire and its object, you are given more and more desires to be fulfilled. You cannot take one desire and fulfill it. Instead, it will multiply into millions of other desires, and they will stand before you also. No one has ever fulfilled desire by fulfilling it!

Renunciation then?

What do you possess that you are going to renounce? What belongs to you that you are able to renounce?

All these desires.

Yes. These desires are not your nature. They don't belong to you.

But they are there.

If they are there, either fulfill them one by one or abandon them. See what suits you.

Have you seen anyone, in the six billion people, who has fulfilled their desires? Have you come across any man who said, "I am content. I have no more desires. I have fulfilled my desires!"—from king to peasant?

So what to do?

The wise man realizes that abandonment of desires is fulfillment of desires. Because when you take up a desire to be fulfilled, it does not give you lasting happiness. So you pick up another desire; again, it does not give you happiness.

To fulfill a desire you need happiness. Love and happiness. You—just for this instant—abandon this concept that fulfilling a desire will make you happy. Let them wait. Abandon all desires, and in the next instant where do you jump? Is it suffering or is it happiness? [*pause*]

We are speaking about renunciation. You renounce for the time being, for just this one moment. You renounce for the time being—as a test, renounce. You can pick up the baggage later; it doesn't matter. In just this moment, spend time on you. If it doesn't suit you, go back again! Just have no link with this queue of desires for some time.

If this queue is broken, the future queue also breaks, because the future is the past itself. Unless you are in the past, you cannot think of the future. So have no relation with the past or the future. Just for a moment. This very instant! Just one second out of your eighty-year span of life. Spend just one second and see what the result is. See for yourself.

In this moment nothing is there.

Okay. Then you have done it. I am very happy. Then I can speak to you, if you've done it.

This moment is not related to the previous queue, to the previous moment. In this moment, you said nothing is there. If nothing is there, where is the suffering? Suffering is when you are with somebody else. Suffering is there when another one is there. Only then, because there is a fear of separation. When you meet a person, where there are two, there is fear and suffering. Why? Separation.

When you say, "In this moment there is nothing," stay in this moment! Look around and tell me, is it a moment of peace and love and beauty, or not?

Everything is quiet. But I can still feel in the background the fear that the old desires will come back again.

This means you will have something better than this moment to give you peace.

Better?

Another thing will come and you will jump out of this peace, jump back into something else, which is already in the queue, that you previously rejected because it didn't give you peace. Will you be so foolish as to give up this love, this peace, for anything else? Even, my dear man, kings have rejected their queens, their treasures, their kingdoms for peace. They go into the forest. Why?

How can you say that, in this moment, there is peace and quietness, and then you want to go back into the garbage?

I don't know.

If you don't know, then you haven't touched That. You have not touched that moment which I have been speaking about. Have no link with the past, no link with the future, and look unto thee in between.

You have understood it intellectually. It is not to understand; it is to plunge into.

For desires you need a body and you need other bodies. You are sitting on a tree which is burning. It is not safe for a bird to stay on it. When the tree is burning, every bird will reject that tree and fly away. How do you keep sitting when there is fire all around? How do you not see the fire? You are sleeping. So wake up!

Lust, anger, and greed are the fire. Has anyone escaped this fire?

***

I like the emptiness you lead us into during satsang, but this can't be the end. Buddha and Osho said there was more.

If there is somewhere further to go, it is not ultimate. Ultimate is here. There is no road, no location, no destination. This is the ultimate truth.

You don't have to travel, you don't have to come or go anywhere. Nothing ever happened. Nothing has to happen. Nothing is happening. This is the ultimate truth.

If there is any road, it must be a concept. Location and destination are concepts. Buddha is a concept. To create all this you must first create your own body. Then you create all these personalities you speak about. First the creation of your body, then the bodies of others.

So where is the mind? Where does it come from? With this question, everything shatters. No beings, no trouble, no bondage, no enlightenment, and no practice to win enlightenment.

If anyone speaks of bondage and ways to achieve enlightenment, I do not know anything about it. In truth there has to be no concept of any body or any being whatsoever.

When the mind arises, everything arises. The Buddha will arise, the bodhi tree will arise, and enlightenment will arise. Find out who the Buddha is.

***

What are the factors that need to be directed to the supreme abode of Being, awareness, and bliss?

These factors are mind, breath, and intellect. That is all you have. Every wise man knows these factors give him peace or suffering.

When directed to something unreal—objects that are transient, not permanent, not real—there is suffering. Ultimately, whichever direction they are moving, they only find Being, awareness, and bliss.

When you become attached to some object outside, it is the bliss or the peace that you seek. But you don't find it, because this object is the creation, the reflection of your own mind. It really does not exist.

Suppose you see your own shadow, and you fall in love with it. It will not help. You have to find the true Being and direct it toward its source. Then there is peace, bliss, and awareness.

Just as the sun painted on a wall will not give you light, reflections of your own mind, manifest as external objects, will never give you peace. You have to turn for light toward the source, not a painted picture of a sun or a candle.

The mind, breath, and intellect have to be directed toward their source. Only then is there peace and rest.

Then Being, awareness, bliss will take the form of the guru, the teacher, the master, who can teach you knowledge of the Self. There cannot be any other teacher other than Being, awareness, bliss.

If you leave this, you will pick up an object. Through objects you cannot win peace or love or freedom.

How to do it? You have to turn toward the source: where the bliss is, where the freedom is, where being is. You have to turn away from your reflected, projected images.

How to do it? Just keep still. Purified intellect. Chaste intellect. A purified mind will be able to return to its source. When you are occupied with objects—"I want this and that"—this takes you away from the source.

What you really want is peace and love. From where you come is where you will return to and where you are. Only your crazy mind, impure intellect, and vasanas are troubling you. You must keep quiet and be still in the satsang of your own Self. Still the mind; keep the intellect very sharp. A tainted intellect will never understand.

***

Don't think, and your own Atman, Para-atman, will act as your own guru—and you are not other than him. You only think so because of the delusion of millions of years of old habits of playing the game. Now, it is enough! Let us return home.

***

When I hear you say, "Drop all names and forms," I go into a panic.

Why do you panic?

Because I try to get it. I think I should do it.

No, no. There are two kinds of panics. One, you have pain because you are losing name and form, and you want to hold on to name and form. You have panic not to hold on to name and form.

Another panic can arise when you hear that you are neither name nor form. Which kind is this? Are you afraid to hear that you are formless?

Yes. I think I'm afraid of dying in that—

Okay, now it's clear. You are afraid that when you have no name and no form, you will die. Then there is panic.

When you are going to sleep at night, do you panic when you drop all name and form? Say at 11p.m. you are going to sleep. At 10:59 and 59 seconds, you are all right? No panic?

You may be with beautiful, beloved friends, in the company of beautiful nature, waterfalls, and forests. You may be in the same bed, but now you are going to separate. Not just separate from friend or body, but from all name and form.

Why do you sleep? Because it gives you rest, gives you peace of mind. If you don't rest for several consecutive nights, you will be somewhere else, but not in satsang. If you don't sleep, if you don't make use of this formless state for several days in a row, your mind is very disturbed. Therefore, you have to sleep. This means you have to forget name and form. In the morning you may say, "I slept very well. I didn't dream a single dream. I don't remember anything." Who was aware of the absence of name and form and is still happy? Who enjoyed nameless and formless state? During sleep you say you were not aware. Who was aware of this sleep? Find out now.

Let me tell you how you are missing. Let me tell you how you are being robbed blind, every time. If you are always thinking, you will go mad. Do you know? People who are mad, paranoid, schizophrenic, are always thinking.

There is even a break between two thoughts to give you rest. What is this rest between two thoughts or two breaths? Nature is always bringing you back to rest and telling you to take rest, but you don't know. You don't hear the advice of your Supreme Mother. Rest is very natural, and you don't look at it.

I gave you three points: sleep, between dreaming and awaking; the distance between thought and thought; and the distance between breath and breath. So breathe in, stop, and look. Inhaling has stopped. At that point, tell me who you are. Who is the person aware of this point?

At this point you renounce everything to know your Self. From birth to death you have lived for others. Even before birth your parents were expecting you. When you were born you already belonged to them.

Can you spare just a few moments solely for yourself? Leave all definition behind. Immediately upon birth, you were already possessed. Then some priest came to initiate you into his fold or sect. You then belonged to that religion.

In truth, you are not only son of God, you are God itself. But who knows this religion? In truth, you have no concept of religion at all. You are pure, immaculate, conscious Self. Freedom itself.

Somebody imposes a religion on you, and you accept it quite well. You say, "I am such and such, and I belong to this fold."

You are eternally free. You have no fold and no sect at all. Then you become a student, then a wife, then a mother of children. Now the time is coming for the evening of life. When you fall sick, the doctor says, "You are my patient."

Death. And then even the mourners claim, "This is my corpse." What a joke!

After that is the grave. In all of this span of life you have not given one instant of time solely for yourself. How can you be happy? Therefore, samsara is there. It is going to stay. As real as anything! Because, mind you, this is your own projection. This is your own ghost. A ghost is very real to a child, not to a wise man. The ghost of samsara is true. This suffering is true.

You have to make a decision eventually. This human birth is a very lucky time. How many ants are there? How many fishes, mosquitoes? Just six billion human beings. And out of six billion, very few will desire freedom. Others will be lost.

Those few who desire freedom come to satsang. Then some of them decide, "Why not have a dance on the road?" They then lose their strength of mind again. They will lose this game because their decision was not correct. Their choice was not a good choice. Not strong. This choice must be a very strong choice: "Here and now, I have to win freedom."

I don't give you any hard work. I don't give you any sadhana or practice. I don't give you any book to learn. Just keep quiet. That's all. And if you don't win freedom, then complain. Come to me and complain to me and say, "I was quiet and it didn't work." Okay?

***

Whenever you start to do something, there must be some desire lurking in the mind.

So I see the washermen washing clothes. How do I clean my mind?

You want a washing machine for your mind? [*laughter*]

Yes.

This washing machine is satsang. The aim of satsang is to burn up the residues of your karmas, which unendingly pull you back into birth and death.

***

When that process is done, there is still some unit that is watching. Some ghost that needs removing.

From within consciousness the idea comes, "I am conditioned." Conditioned in the unconditioned limitlessness. Even in the depths, you have to go deeper. Fathomlessness means you have to keep on plunging. When you remove everything you will find there is some original dark point.

Once upon a time, mind was, herself, unconditioned consciousness. Conditioned consciousness is still consciousness. The mind and consciousness have the same color. So how to remove this conditioning? Wherever you are there will be some conditioning. You arrive at any depth and there will still be some conditioning. What conditioning? You must further transcend. You will be involved in many subtle stages. Beyond physical, vital, subtle, and so on.

***

How do I find intuition?

For intuition, dive within yourself. Dive within, now. Then allow intuition to work, instead of the mind. The mind needs tuition and tutor. Therefore, when you direct your mind toward its source and do not think, intuition [prajna] will rise and work much better than thinking. It will take charge of your mind, intellect, senses, objects, and daily routine.

First you must return. Direct your mind to the source and do not think. That is the prescription for wisdom, for intuition.

"I will do this." "I want to do that." "I have decided this." This is called mental gymnastics and it leads to suffering. Try both ways. First try "I will do." Then, let the Supreme Power—who is responsible for all manifestation, who is responsible for giving light to the sun, who is responsible for giving power to the earth, for growing food—let that power look after you.

"I can do it" is arrogance and pride. If you don't return back to your Supreme Mother, who has sent you here for a different purpose, you have lost track. No harm. Still time. You can still do it.

Your absolute desire to return home is the only requirement to be fulfilled. It will reveal itself instantly, then and there.

The children are making sandcastles on the beach. They get lost in their play and they don't want to return home. But their parents say, "It is now evening. Let's go home."

The parents remind them, and the children kick their sandcastles. They equally enjoy knocking them down and building them up. Without any loss or suffering, they go back home.

Night is falling. You can't stay in your sand house. There will be high tide in the night. You can't stay. The high tide will wash away all your plans and houses.

So before the high tide, better to return to a safe place.

TRAP OF THE SENSES

Everybody wants to be free. What is the one impediment between you and freedom? Craving. Desire or expectation for something which is perishable.

You are devoted to that craving. Thus, you are devoted to this manifestation and its construction; craving that which is impermanent leads to suffering, old age, and death.

Everyone is involved in this craving for sense pleasures, and it has not given peace to anyone. No one, from king to middle-class to workers, is happy. They are all chasing what appears and disappears.

Craving for what is not real takes you away from the eternal reality. Gods have everything, but still they are not happy.

You always have a light within you, but you don't turn toward it. Instead, you see this light shining on outer objects. You chase these objects, looking for the light. But you are only seeing reflections of the light within. You run looking for satisfaction from the objects that have caught the reflection of your inner light.

You are hunting outside. This is called craving.

When you decide, "Enough! I must be free," then the function of the mind stops going out and clinging to objects in search of happiness. It becomes no-mind. The mind is only mind in the fulfillment of its desires. When you desire something, when you crave something, when you expect something, then it takes this function, and its name is mind.

Stop it, and it is quiet. In this quietness, you can't call it mind. So dam the flow of the river flowing outward. Energy is not being wasted then. When it is dammed, it stops. Then it is quiet. In this quietness, the river will be no river. You can't call it a river now. Now call it a reservoir.

This reservoir, without ripples, is identical to your own light. This light is inside your mind.

Now the mind is no-mind. No mind, no craving, no expectations, no desires, no notions, and no ideas.

It is good to stop. Then you will see that you have found the precious stone you have been seeking. Having found this, you will be happy. You will be satisfied. You don't expect anything more, because this is chitdarman, the fulfillment of all desires. Chitdarman means you just think and it happens. Chitdarman, the precious stone which shines by its own luster.

How to keep it?

This is a precious stone. Having it, you have everything. How can you lose it? Only by having a fear that it can be lost and then wanting to keep it.

You have not lost it. Having found that precious stone which is hidden inside of you, burning, how can you lose it?

It is shining by its own luster. Because your attention is somewhere else, it is reflected on objects, and this reflection attracts you to the objects. This attraction is not wisdom.

Instead, find out where this beauty, this shine, this luster, this reflection, is coming from. Why not go there? You will turn your face from the object which is being reflected and shown. You will go on the other side, where this luster is coming from. There, you will see that this shine has always been there, and it is yours. It is you itself. How are you going to lose it?

Merge into the light, and you are the light. You are the precious stone. How can you lose your own Self?

Everything—kingdoms, worlds, relationships—can be lost, and will be lost. Even your own body you will lose some day. If you can't even depend upon your own body or mind, what can you depend upon?

Therefore, patiently, wisely, allow some time by yourself and think about it. "Have these things that I have possessed so far given me peace of mind?" All the belongings and all the relations. I don't think anybody can say yes.

Everybody is losing every minute. Every minute there are millions of people dying and millions taking birth. Every minute this is continuing. We are here today and may not be tomorrow. This breath can leave at any time.

Therefore, true wisdom is the desire to find the precious stone and declare, " I will win it today, without delay!" Then you will see that you don't have to find it. It has its own luster. You are not to take your own lamp. It shines by its own light. You only have to turn your face toward it.

Luster is here, but your eyes are not clean. You can't see it here in the water by the bed of the river. You can't see it because there is dust in your eyes. What is the dust? Desire.

Remove this dust, this desire, this craving, this expectation. If you remove this dust of desire and expectation, what do you see?

Emptiness.

Emptiness! [*laughs*] If there is dust, there is manifestation, never-ending sorrow and suffering. Remove this dust instantly and see for five minutes.

Make a decision: "In this entire life cycle, I will give five minutes to remove the dust from my eyes." And then see! You will see face-to-face your own face!

Swaroopam. This is called darshan. Your own Swaroopam.

Nobody sees. Everybody sees other faces! Not their own. With dust in your eyes, you will only see otherness. No dust, no otherness. All your own Self, your own reflections. Nobody else. No stranger.

This is called removing the dust. First, "I am this and he is that." This is dust. When the dust is removed, there is no *you,* no *I,* and no *she.* Get rid of craving, expectation, and desire. You won't lose anything.

Go straightaway and see your own Self. See the freedom, the consciousness. Later on it will be seen what you don't have. Leave off all practices. Later on we will see what we have to do. Straightaway, go and see your own Self.

Then if you need any practice, do it. If, before seeing, you fall into the trap of any practice, you will not see the Self. Instead, you will stay there and be so attached to what you are doing that you will say, "This is all," and you will forget to seek further, to your own Self.

Forget everything! Forget all attachments. Forget freedom and forget bondage. There is no wall between you and consciousness. It is just your playing because you don't want to proceed further.

You have come here for freedom, not for anything else. Keep freedom always in mind.

***

Do I have to give up women to be free?

It was a woman who gave you birth. Your own mother. Household life has nothing to do with freedom. This is a totally different affair. So far as I have seen, going off to a monastery doesn't benefit anyone either.

But I make love with other women, not my wife.

Then you are her problem. If you look to another woman and you are no problem to your wife, and she does the same and it is no problem to you—if you have this agreement, there is no problem.

Well, she doesn't agree.

That's what I said: you are her problem. You say you are a swami. What is the meaning of swami? Someone who has given up all desires, here and beyond also—a very respectable name. If you are a swami, you have to behave properly.

Happiness is not about fulfilling desires for some object, like sex. It is only when this desire terminates that happiness is possible. Desirelessness gives you happiness. Whenever desire arises, look within to where the desire is arising from, and when this desire vanishes, you will experience tremendous happiness.

However, once you gain an object of desire, another one will be there. One fulfilled, and another is waiting. Even kings are not happy. No-desire is absolute bliss. And when you are bliss, then there is peace. When there is peace, then there is stillness of mind. When there is stillness of mind, this is freedom. Satisfaction of desires will never end. Bodies will end. Millions of bodies have ended, and still the thirst for enjoyment of desire is not fulfilled. Therefore, we are hitchhiking from incarnation to incarnation. So do whatever you want.

***

If you accidentally catch fire due to an accident, and you are rushing to jump into the river, and a friend comes by and says, "Let's go to a restaurant and get some ice cream," what will you do? This desire for freedom must be like this. You do not stop along the way to pick up another desire.

***

Sound, sight, smell, taste, and touch—you are encircled by these five senses where the fire enters. And what is the fire? Desire. It is burning and you are sleeping. Wake up! Here and now.

You are surrounded by these five windows through which the fire enters your house. And you are snoring. What is this fire, what are these windows? Your desires.

This human birth is a supreme vehicle for freedom. How you differ from other animals is that you have a chance to get freedom. So look where the fire is entering! Through sound, sight, smell, taste, and touch—these are the five fires. You have to check these desires.

All other animals are destroyed by just one fire. The moth is drawn to a candle by sight. Desire for enjoyment of light is the supreme desire of the moth, and it takes him to the flame where he perishes.

Just one taste, and the fish is caught on the hook.

Deer are attracted by sound, and they are caught.

The way to catch elephants is to dig a large hole. On this hole, spread straw, and make an effigy of a female elephant standing on the straw. Elephants come to touch the other and get caught.

The bee goes to the flower by smell, and some flowers catch the bee for food.

All these perish by just one fire, and you have five fires. You have to be very careful. Check your desires, and you will be firmly established in the Self, by the Self, within the Self. This can be won in this very instant.

What is needed is only the very firm decision "I want freedom." That is enough. All other desires—even gods cannot get rid of them, let alone us men.

***

There once lived a rishi. His wife was the most beautiful woman in the world. This rishi was living in the forest with his wife. His wife was very devoted to him. News spread about her beauty, even to the region of the gods.

The three gods, Brahma, Vishnu, and Mahesh, were attracted to see the beauty of this woman. So they descended in the form of sanyassins. [When a sanyassin stands at the door, he has to be attended to first, before anything else. The host must always go out and see what he wants.]

At this time the woman was in the bathroom. The gods chose this moment because it was the right occasion to see her beauty, as she was in the bathroom and she had to come immediately. She could not even take time to dress herself, which was their intention.

This woman heard the voices outside the door while she was in the bath. What to do? She had to rush out to see the three sanyassins. Brahma, Vishnu, and Mahesh are involved in seeing a naked woman. Creator, Preserver, and Destroyer, in the guise of sanyassins.

Through the power of her tapas, she converted the gods into six-month-old children. She brought all three gods, as six-month-old babies, into the house, put them in a cradle, and began swinging them.

The gods hadn't told their wives that they were going on this mission to earth. Even though their own wives were beautiful women, the gods had felt compelled to go to earth.

Kamila, Uma, and Ramanyi were searching here and there for their husbands. They went to a famous siddha and, by his yogic power, he saw the gods' whereabouts. He told the wives where their husbands were.

They went to the rishi's wife. "We hear our husbands are in your ashram."

"Yes, come see them."

The wives were brought in to see their husbands as babies, sucking their thumbs. All the goddesses prostrated before this woman. The gods then turned back into their adult forms and kissed her feet. This is the power of tapas.

All of you have this power, if you lock these windows where the fire enters. The fire enters only when you desire. This desire is fire. Check the desires. Enough desires! For millions of years you have been seeking the fulfillment of these desires, one incarnation after the other.

***

If you are fed up, then you burn to stop and look for something unknown. To be free, to get enlightenment, liberation, you need a very firm decision.

Do it with the Self, by the Self, within the Self, in this very instant. Self is not far away. What is the delay? Only desire.

Abandon all desires, and you will be the happiest person on this planet, and perhaps you will help people on other planets also. But first help yourself. First know yourself, who you are. Then there will be no fires. There will be no desires.

The only desire worth achieving is the desire for freedom. All other desires are worthless. They have not given you any happiness, any peace. All this mischief! All is burning. All three worlds are burning. The heavens are burning; gods are burning. Even gods descended to earth to see this beautiful woman. And her true beauty was the inner purity of Self.

***

Everything depends upon you. If you want to postpone it, postpone it for a few more years or incarnations, but that is not the way of a wise man. A wise man takes the opportunity at hand. He does not become deluded by ignorance.

Freedom is here and now, this very instant. What you have to do is stop linking your mind with the past moment, stop linking your mind with a future moment. No connection with the past and no connection with the future. I am speaking of these three moments now. A moment is the very minutest measure of time. Don't give rise to past or future.

Look into this very instant. All past and future is just the mind which has been cheating you. The mind is a ghost, a name only. When there is mind, all this manifestation is there with one thought. When you are established in this non-moment, when there is no past, this place is called no-mind.

Yesterday somebody asked, "How do I carry on with my routine if I don't desire?" Here is the answer once again. This moment is no-mind. And no-mind has the same qualities as emptiness. No-mind is consciousness itself, Self itself.

This no-mind is very sattvic. It has transcended past and present and future to be no-mind. No-mind is consciousness. There is no more mind at all now. The purified mind is consciousness.

What is purification of mind? No thought. This thoughtless mind, sattvic mind, no-mind, can be called consciousness itself. Self itself. Get firmly established in this nature. You do not even ask for freedom, because freedom was only in the mind, tired with suffering and bondage.

Therefore, the mind itself suggests going to satsang. If you have no relation with the past or future, there is no mind at all, and you are home. Look within the Self, by the Self.

All the rest is with the body and mind, and all results will be mental or physical. Here, question the mind with itself: "Who are you?" With just this question, the mind will disappear, and this mind will be very happy in her own dissolution. The mind will be very grateful to have this peace. The mind has been jumping from one branch to another branch, like a monkey. Neither it nor you were at rest. Freedom is here and now.

Your nature is pure freedom. You were free from the beginning. How did this idea come into your mind that you are bound? Where are the chains? Have you seen them?

Simply ask yourself, "Who am I?" This is a raft to cross over the ocean of samsara. Death cannot enter this raft. This is such a safe raft. All else is the mind: "I will do this." "I want that." "What should I do?" "I have this." "I will have that." All notions and intentions. Stop everything for a while. Not much time is needed.

You have not given attention to this. When a thought arises in your mind, check it. Be vigilant! Keep vigilance over the arising of the thought.

***

To stay at home, what path is needed? Desire gives rise to a path to lead you away from home. Desire for anything that is not permanent is the thief who robs you of peace and happiness. If you have any desire, make it the desire to know who you are.

Sanyas means "no attachment to, or desire for, anything which is not permanent." So sanyas should happen when you have satisfied yourself, when all desires and experiences of the objects of the senses have not given you any benefit, any peace, any love.

Rejection of all desire is sanyas. Changing clothes is not it. Changing circumstances is not it. The mind is still not changed. Changing circumstances from one place to another, one country to another, is not sanyas. Sanyas is getting rid of all desire. This will stop the cycle of birth and death, and give you peace.

If you stop the hub, the wheel stops. What is the hub? The mind. How to stop the mind? Inquire, "Who am I?" If you say, "What is this?" or "Who are you?" you will get some response, and the mind will abide on some object of the senses.

Ask this question: "Who am I?" Instead, people ask, "What about my duties and daily functions?"

You are chained by your outlook, so look within. This inquiry is not related to any past or future thought. Not giving rise to any thought is called sanyas. If I dye my clothes, or go to Poona, the mind goes along. The mind must take sanyas, giving up all desire for sense objects, and turn within to meet its source.

You may fool the people by the color of your clothes and the rosaries hanging around your neck, but the mind is still the same. Let the mind take sanyas. Question the mind: "Who are you? Who has been troubling me all these millions of years?"

***

To be happy, to be at peace, to be love, to be beauty, you do not need anyone else. To be otherwise, you need some thought, some idea, or some person to give you unhappiness. Some person must be the source of unhappiness—some person, some idea, or some thing.

Happiness doesn't ask anything of you. But to suffer you must make some effort at relationship. You must refer to some relationship with a person, thing, or idea in order to suffer. Then you get unhappy because you need something. To be happy is your fundamental nature. Nothing is needed. You don't need any help to be happy. To suffer you need some relationship. And where is the relationship in the world that does not give you suffering?

I don't know.

If you don't know, perhaps you have heard of one from your parents? [*laughs*]

***

I have stopped everything, and now I feel like I've lost my vitality.

Stopping your desires is your nature. It is your nature to have no desires. This is not a loss. When you are born, the very first hour, what was your desire?

To breathe.

Okay, to breathe. And this breathing was not yours. It was not your effort. Now you are breathing. Tell me, how many breaths do you breathe in one day, or even in one minute?

I don't know.

You don't know because it is not your effort. It is going on. Air from outside is returning inside. It reaches our nose and we call it prana, as if it belongs to us. Same air, inhaling or exhaling. This life force is you! Find out: Do you command this life force? Or does the life force command you?

The life force commands me.

Yes, the life force commands you. You are breathing. The art of breathing is effortless. You make an effort not to breathe, and see the result. At death, a very rich man cannot buy one extra breath. No doctor can give one breath extra. Who is breathing inside of you? Who is sucking the air from outside to inside?

Once sucked, the body is working—the mind, the brain, and the senses are working and transacting business between subject and object and having pleasures. Find out who is responsible for this, and you will find the answer to your question.

Who is hidden, unknown and hidden, within the cave of your heart? This is your own real face, your most intimate friend, and this is eternal. Nobody looks at it. "I am doing this." "I have done that." "I will do this." That is called life, and nobody is happy and contented with what he has done. He always wants to do something more. He gets happiness, and having gotten it, he wants something else. This is an unending cycle. So stop this cycle, I say. It is not natural to you.

Somehow, the mind has created a problem. So ask the mind. You have tried everything on this planet, from hell to heaven, and still you are not satisfied. Ask your mind and you will get the answer. Your mind is your mind, and he is a very troublesome boy. You have seen it. Everywhere it has bitten you and given you trouble.

So, now, have a dialogue between you and your mind. What do you want? The mind will become your friend. It will show you the way. We want desires fulfilled and we blame the mind. Where is the mind? Who has seen it? It is a ghost, and this ghost is desire. Therefore, stop for an instant. Simply stop and look unto yourself.

I don't ask you to suppress anything. I don't want you to walk away from your daily routines. Perhaps you will respond with 200 percent to your daily activities.

If you are generous, I beg not even a moment, not even a second, just 1/45,000th of a second. Can you give me that much time? See your face—all will be fulfilled. Your treasure is hidden inside, and you run out and away from that. From timelessness, the sun arises which marks your time of day, of sunrise and sunset. It all arises in you.

***

Once there was a king. Vajravalkya was his name. One day he called his two wives together. One was very old and one was a young girl, maybe twenty years of age.

He said, "I am going to divide my kingdom equally between the two of you. You are good queens; everything will be divided in half. The jewelry, the elephants, the palace—all will be divided equally because I am leaving you."

The young queen said, "Isn't it true that you said that I am the light of your life? Didn't you say I was the most beautiful woman in the kingdom and how happy I made you?"

"Well, I know you are a wise man. If you are giving all this up, it must be for something better than this. So you can give my half to the other queen. I want to follow you and go where you are going."

Vajravalkya said it would be hard, that he was only going with one robe. She took off her diamonds and gave them to the other queen and said to her husband, "One sari is enough. I would like to go with you and serve you."

So they went to the forest together to perform austerity. They had satsang all the time. They were very happy and they won freedom.

Papaji, after the king abandons his queen, abandons his desire, if it is truly abandoned, could he be with the queen again, physically?

Yes. They lived as such.

And it's okay?

Yes, they did that. But the foolish desire through the senses is not there. It is love. You are returning from original peace. Everything will be there—wife will be there, husband will be there, friends will be there—but your concept is different now. Only love, no hate, no fear of separation, because then you will have relationship with the Self, with your own Self. In all this, Self is your own Self. Who can you hate?

Beauty everywhere.

Everywhere, yes. When you are everywhere, you see your own face in every Self. Where will you go? What is there to renounce and what is there to reject? This is here, wherever you are.

Find your own peace—first in you, then in me, then everywhere. Look within. Self is not far away. Self is here and now! How far is the Self situated from you?

Same.

It is the same! You don't need to search. Only give up your search for other things. When you give up your search for everything else, what will you be? Give up yourself. Revelation is going to take place by itself, within your own Self!

The only effort that you have to make is the effort to throw away the efforts you have loaded on your own head. An effort may be needed to throw away your own efforts. Don't make any effort toward your own Self. This revelation will take place. You have a bundle of things that you have collected with effort. So, you can make a countereffort to remove your effort. But do not make an effort to be as you are.

It is a recognition. It will reveal itself to you by itself, even if you don't want it. You throw away the bonded things that you have been bonding. Throw away your bonds. Do away with your bonds. Make no effort. It is a revelation itself. It is here, you see.

Just look within yourself; just make up your mind with a firm conviction.

***

Osho said that he regretted only one thing in his life: that he did not meet Ramana Maharshi before leaving his body.

I don't think he has missed it. This is a very good desire. Even after death, this intense desire for the Self to meet the Self will be fulfilled. This is not like other desires: "I want this and I want that." Those desires will get you in trouble, and those objects will manifest in your next incarnation.

Any desire for the Self is a desire which is fulfilled. The body has nothing to do with this desire. Either the body stays or it doesn't stay. This desire is an eternal desire.

Even in the body there is Videha Mukti, Jivan Mukti. Liberation can be won before the end of this body, and it will stay after the body drops.

You can wear this physical garment or shed it—it doesn't matter—but this desire for liberation must stay during your lifetime, and after your lifetime, since this is a desire for truth itself. Truth is eternal. It has to reveal itself, by itself, to itself.

Truth can never be revealed to the body, because the body is not permanent. It cannot stand the darshan of divinity. So shed the concept of the body, and you will have the direct perception of your own Self.

***

Understanding does not take any words. Just allow my words to sink somewhere that is final. As you go to sleep you say goodnight to your closest friend, someone you live with all the waking hours. You say goodnight to everything. You cannot take anything with you or you won't sleep. You must let go of everything.

Do you know who is sleeping next to you when you sleep? Like this, everything is let go. Why good night? Why don't you take him or her with you into the next state? No name and no form, no relationship—and you are happy.

I will tell you a simple trick. Whenever you get rid of anything, you are happy. Don't possess anything. Suppose your neighbor has the latest model Mercedes Benz, and your wife or your husband is troubling you. You think, "I must buy the latest model."

Somehow you borrow money from the bank or your money-market fund, and now the car is in front of your house. You are happy, aren't you?

You must be happy. Your wife is happy; your children are happy; your friends are happy. The person who sold it is happy to get rid of the car. [*laughter*]

And you are happy to have it. Now where is the happiness? This desire was troubling you: "I want a car." With the car, the desire has left you. With the car there is no more desire for a car, and this has given you happiness. As with all desires, you are happy when the desire has vanished, not when the thing has come.

The car is made of steel and rubber and runs on gasoline. None of these elements make you happy.

You are sitting in emptiness, and you think you are the owner because of the walls of the house you are sitting in. You are still in the emptiness. Wherever there is emptiness, you are happy. This is a simple trick.

You forget your body and, empty of body, empty of relations, empty of friends, you slide down into sleep and are happy.

This is the so-called waking state now, but this is also an ignorant state. This ignorant waking state is also a sleep state.

You are sleeping because you are transacting desires. Keep quiet here, and see that you are still sleeping.

When you wake up, this ignorance of sleep disappears. Ignorance is due to illusion. You get rid of illusion through knowledge. As knowledge of a mirage destroys its magic power of appeal, so here you question, "Who am I?" Then slowly you will return back home.

Finally! Get rid of all these illusions permanently!

***

With any desire, there is always some pleasure, no matter how small or fleeting. So it is difficult to give up this pleasure. Therefore, it is difficult to give up desires.

Freedom is not for you, my dear boy. Perhaps wait another cycle. It takes, perhaps, incarnating in 8.4 million species to get to the point of desiring freedom. Spans of time are different. Some incarnations are days, some are minutes, some are hours, some are many years. In all, perhaps thirty-five million years for another cycle, another round.

No problem. Enjoy once more. Freedom is not for you. You are at the wrong place. This is not the fish market, my dear boy. I give you this advice: Go to a fish market to buy fishes. This place is not suitable for you.

This is a very serious business here. You have to be serious. One day you will be ready, either this cycle or next cycle. No problem. When you are very serious, burning for freedom, then come to me. If you want freedom, come to me. You will have freedom. If you have some other craving, I can't help you.

***

Running after the pleasures of the senses is called the waking state. Transaction between subject and object is called the waking state. Imagination of these is called the dream state. Where nothingness is left, not even inquiry, this is called the dull ego state, ignorant sleep state.

When you say, "I want to be free," it is neither waking nor sleeping. This is a transcendental state that comes from nowhere.

If you have unfulfilled desires, you will be reborn in a new womb. That bag of unfulfilled desires will be your face. Appropriate species, parents, and circumstances will appear for this face.

Therefore, fulfill all your desires in one instant. You need only fire to burn this whole store of desires. One desire for enlightenment is the flame. Once enlightened, all your desires are reduced to ashes—no more returning to any womb. Otherwise, you will be forever hitchhiking from place to place.

***

Where there are paths, there must be sheep. Paths are meant for sheep.

Do you see lions walking on a path? And where there are sheep, there are shepherds. When you go to a shepherd, you become a sheep, and they herd you where they want.

When the light came, you did not go to the candle, but outside to the object the light was shining on. This flame is your teacher. Adore it. Seek it. Try to know it. Have no concept of the past, present, or future.

This instant, wait! Stop! Look nowhere! And perhaps everything will be revealed. When you look for a method or a technique, you postpone it. When you postpone, you have been cheated by an intimate friend: mind.

INQUIRY AND DEVOTION

My mind keeps running and tripping me. How do you deal with an active mind?

There are two ways: one way is vichara, or Self-inquiry; the other is devotion.

Inquiry is the question "Who am I?" which takes you to discover the answer. When you ask, "Who am I?" you have no other thoughts. You can have one thought at a time, and you hold on to this thought "Who am I?" When the mind is engaged in this question, you stick to it—absolutely alert. Place full attention on finding the answer to this. No other thought will come, because you are firmly engaged in this inquiry. You start with ego. The ego wants to know "Who am I?" Doesn't it? Thought is ego.

So there is still ego involved?

Of course. Who else is searching? You first felt that you are separate; therefore, you want to return to your original nature; therefore, you make this inquiry.

You have forgotten yourself, and believe in separation. You must overcome this separation. Question who you are, and this will take you to your origin.

From where is the *I* arising? Plunge there. Beyond *I,* you don't know. That place isn't known to anyone. You plunge in and see. This is inquiry. Dive deep into the unknown. Then there is no ego.

This is meant for very sharp, very intelligent people. You are free already, so do not strive or aspire to attain anything whatsoever. Any gain or loss is not eternal, and therefore not worth anything. Any gain will be lost. Anything not here and now is of no use. You must discover what is here and now already. That is your own presence, your own emptiness. So you must return to your original nature and not acquire anything here.

The absolute exalts a holy person. You must present yourself in absolute, immaculate mind. An unsmelled flower has to be offered to God.

You need not read a book nor take up a practice. This is the beginning and the end at the same time. Instantly you will get it.

In your presence, in this moment, I feel it.

This *I* is ego. Ego is striking at its own root. When she turns back and sees her mother, she will be dissolved in shame. Because ego has been boasting all along, I will create the whole universe. I will do this. I will do that. This belongs to me.

This is a foolproof method. No other way will take you to enlightenment; all other ways are confusions. This is the ultimate way.

Another way, equally good—as a bird needs two wings to fly—is devotion. My background is devotion—

Really? That's amazing. I was just speaking to this swami who also says his way is devotion. He opens himself to the love of Ramakrishna and Jesus and Buddha, and purifies himself in that love.

In devotion none of that is necessary.

How does devotion work then?

In devotion you surrender to the Supreme. You do nothing but surrender to the Supreme, who will look after everything, as it does even now.

Your speaking of God brings great joy.

Yes. [*begins to cry*] Whatever you speak of, the mind is there. You speak of a rose, the mind goes there. Like that. [*crying*] This is why I rarely use this word "devotion" in satsang.

Why not?

If I hear of devotion, there will be no satsang. This word takes you there, as you said.

First is the actual surrender; then it takes care of you. "Let thy will be done. I have no will," will be your expression.

I don't stay stabilized. Can you help me? To stay in that presence is my greatest desire.

When you surrender there is no desire, just as a moth looks at the flame. The moth is in love with the flame. It is attracted to the flame, and it wants to kiss its love. This desire takes it to the flame. That's all, and there is no return. Like this, surrender, and everything will be taken care of by

God itself. This is already the case, but we don't accept it. We are so arrogant to say, "I do this thing."

The next minute is not guaranteed. Everyone is boasting, "I did that. I will do that tomorrow." Who has seen tomorrow? Surrender to God, and leave everything to him. This is instant freedom.

When you have sold your mind to someone else, you have nothing to offer to God. If you offer your heart to God, the kingdom of heaven is opened unto you, whether you want it or not.

Do you have to choose one path or the other?

Devotion is ultimately going to take you to inquiry as well. At first it looks like devotee, devotion, and God.

In the surrender, the devotee merges into the divine itself, and then there is no more devotion. It comes from and returns to the same source.

There are external symptoms of devotion: tears and choking of the voice. You are accepted by the divine, and these symptoms come. You are accepted. Very nice.

I was mad for the divine. People called it mad. So much divine ecstasy. Who can speak? This is why I can't speak of this in satsang. I choke and can't speak.

Did you feel free with devotion?

Surrender is freedom. No mind left! No separation is left. Love of God is freedom. The name of God alone is enough. No difference between the name of God and God. Consciousness, emptiness, enlightenment, God—same.

***

There is no past in the eyes of a Jivan Mukta [liberated soul]. No past, no present, and no future. Just things as they are. No time, no sun, no moon, no stars. Just tremendous peace.

As you think, so it will become. This is the beauty of consciousness.

It is consciousness; it does not need to borrow material from anywhere else. "Let there be manifestation," and manifestation is there. Whatever you think is instantly there, within consciousness. Consciousness desiring for whatever it is within consciousness.

Nothing has ever happened. Nothing is ever going to happen. This is ultimate truth. Everything else is trouble of the mind.

When mind arises, trouble arises. You have to check at the arising point of the mind itself. You just stay there, where the mind is arising. Mind is a thought. *I* arises, everything arises. Before *I,* people report that they don't see anything, which is peace, beauty, love.

If, after you see your own source, your own peace, you give rise to a single thought, the past, present, and future instantly arise. When you dream, you instantly see a mountain or an elephant. Because all is consciousness. Even when you do not know, you are conscious of not knowing. When you say, "I am suffering," you are conscious of suffering.

The only way to get rid of suffering is inquiry. This inquiry, or vichara, is a raft to cross the ocean of samsara to reach nirvana. This raft—wherever you are: eating, sleeping, or walking—this raft is very safe. Nothing can touch you. This inquiry will throw you out of the mind. Just keep quiet, and see that no thought touches you for this moment.

***

How do I keep going in?

You have to leave everything behind. To go in, you leave behind mind, ego, body, senses, and manifestation. All of that is not here in that instant of going in. Also, *I* is not here.

That's right.

I means mind. Mind means ego; ego means senses; senses means manifestation. So this inquiry is at the root of the ego, and you say you have done it.

Yes, but only for a moment.

Agreed! So lift up a step from this presence, and plant a foot somewhere. Where will you plant it?

I must try not to think about that.

You can think, do whatever you do. You have landed in the ocean. Do whatever you want: think, talk, swim.

But how do I let go, to go in?

You said you did it!

For the instant of no-time.

Agreed! From that no-time, you now want to go to time.

No, I don't. I want to let go.

Time is mind, and time is past.

I know.

For this instant of no-time, you said you went out of time. Now I want you to walk out of timelessness!

Ah...

Now you have nothing to do. Ah—that's it, now you've got it. Don't think for this, or make any effort, and you are here. You will always be here, and you have always been here, but you were otherwise occupied. [*laughs*]

The past is a graveyard. All your tears and suffering must come from the past. If you unceasingly search for who you are, there will be no room for the past to come into consciousness. You are already occupied. Then there is no space for the past.

First you disappear; then you will dive into the ocean of ambrosia. Then whatever you speak will be poetry. Then there is no one speaking.

***

When I go inside, I feel my heartbeat getting stronger.

Ignore it! Your real heart is neither inside nor outside. Concentrate on That. Where will you concentrate?

The real heart is reality. It is the substratum of the world. Reality, untouched. When you have peace, you have a direct relation with that heart. When you are relating or concentrating on that heart which is neither inside nor outside, you are in peace. This state is not waking, sleeping, or dreaming. This is a state which is your own Being. This is a transcendental state. When this state is mature, it will be your own state, and this state will lead you to freedom. And you will have peace.

When you realize your natural state, it is here. All this manifestation is a cosmic playground, and you are the dancer. Then there is no acceptance and no rejection. This is freedom, enlightenment. This is already here, but you are otherwise engaged.

You impose the notion of activity—"I am doing this, I will do that"—on the substratum of inactivity. There is something inactive that doesn't work at all. From there arises the notion of activity, and you get involved in activity.

If you then attach to certain things, you are lost.

If you know where this activity arises from, that it arises from nonaction, from the non-activated, you will realize freedom. Then action won't lodge in your memory; therefore, no karma. No karma means all notions of world cycle are over.

When you concentrate and yet don't make any effort, it will show up by itself. Disturbance is your thought. Your nature is peace. Just keep quiet, and see that no thought arises. When no thought arises, this is peace. Thought is always going to the past and the future, and this is called world cycle and suffering. Don't do anything, and see how peace comes to you.

Only this thought wave is disturbing the calmness of the ocean.

***

In truth, everything is included in devotion. You are not left at all, even to think. In surrender, there is no thinking. You can't demand or command. The river surrenders to the ocean with no trace. It is like this. We are discharging our love to God, not to anybody else. Love must be for the eternal friend, not for things which come and go.

Since you were already in devotion to God, what did you get when you met Ramana Maharshi?

Vichara. This I never knew. Now I speak about it because now I have realized. My master used to speak about this, and through his grace, I received the experience. My master gave me this experience.

I was in devotion, but something was missing. There was still a separation which was unbearable. I used to dance with Krishna, but not twenty-four hours. Sometimes there was separation, and this was very painful. I wanted to have it stabilized twenty-four hours. Until then, I didn't have a teacher.

I went all over India in search of a guru. I would ask, "Have you seen God? And if you have, can you enable me? And what is your charge? I will serve you all the rest of this life." Everybody said, "You have to do practice."

But I said, "No. When I go to the market, I see what I want and I pay. It should be like this. I am willing to pay, but do you have what I want? Why should I practice?"

They would say I am mad. The gurus' students would rise up and say, "We have been here for forty years. We have grown gray beards and still we have not yet found the way. So stay here and practice."

"But I have not come for that. If the guru has seen God, what is the problem in his showing it to me?" I went everywhere, searching without result.

Then I went home, disappointed. My father was quite upset because I was not working. One day I was sitting in a house, and a sadhu came for alms, bhiksha.

I said, "Swamiji, you can have lunch with me. You have been traveling throughout India. Can you give me the address of someone who has seen God?"

He said, "Oh yes, I know one person. Go to him." So he gave me the address of Ramana Maharshi. He lives in Tiruvannamalai, south of Madras.

I noted the address, and he left. I had no money, and my father would give me no money, as he was already taking care of my wife and children. I was very shy to borrow money. I had helped people, but I had not taken money from anyone else.

I had one friend who was a sweetmeat merchant. We had done gymnastics together in boyhood. He invited me to his place for some milk. There was an old newspaper lying on the table. I started casually looking at the want-ad column.

I saw an advertisement for an ex-army officer to work in Madras. I applied, got money and a travel ticket to Madras, and one month's time to report.

I went from the Punjab to Madras, and then to Ramanashram. I got down from the bullock cart, and was guided and told that the saint was there in the hall. I went and saw it was the same sadhu who had given me the address.

I got very angry and did not enter the hall. I thought this was the same man who was boasting about himself. I wanted to go back to the station.

A man who lived in the ashram followed me outside and asked, "Aren't you from the north? You have come all this way. Why not stay some time?"

I told him, "No. This man is a fraud. He gave me his own address; therefore, I don't want to see him or to stay."

The man said, "No, you are making a mistake. It cannot be him. He has not moved from here for fifty years. He came here as a boy. He must have shown himself to you by his special powers."

I didn't agree, but he insisted and took my baggage and gave me a room. Straightaway, there was a bell for lunch. The maharishi was there in the hall for lunch, and I saw clearly that he was the same person I had met in Punjab. I decided to speak to him anyway.

After lunch everybody left, and he went back into the hall. I didn't know that after lunch, nobody went to see him. I went into the hall, and the caretaker stopped me because this was the maharishi's time for rest. But

Maharishi was looking at me, and signaled me to come.

I spoke to him and said, "Are you not the same person who met me in Punjab fifteen days ago?" He just kept quiet.

I said, "I don't understand silence. Please speak." He didn't speak. Even then, I was not happy with him. I was not happy with this silence which I had never heard.

Anyway, I thought, this place is nice. It is very attractive, very holy. Since I am here anyway, I will go to the other side of the hill. I hiked alone four miles from the ashram, seeking my Krishna.

After a while, it was time to leave and return to Madras to start my work. I came to say goodbye to Maharishi. He said, "You have not come to see me."

I said, "No, I was living on the other side of the hill, and now I am going to Madras."

He asked me, "What have you been doing?"

I said with pride, "I was playing with my Krishna."

He said, "Very good. You have been seeing Krishna?"

"Yes," I said proudly.

"Do you see him now?"

"No. Now I don't. When I have a vision, I see him. Now I don't."

He then said, "So Krishna appeared and disappeared?"

He said, "What appeared has disappeared. The seer is still here. God cannot be an object that appears and disappears. So find out who the seer is."

For the first time ever, I heard, "Find out who the seer is."

With the master, I got the experience. This experience was already here. When we love God, we think he is an object. But he is the subject. So you have to surrender to the subject. The ego is the object.

You merge into the subject so that no object is left behind. God will speak, God will walk, and God will see. I got this from my master. I saw the seer. I realized the seer through my master, and prostrated myself before him.

Then I returned to Madras to take up my duty. All holidays, Saturdays, and Sundays, I would return to Tiruvannamalai to spend with him. It was so close, only four hours. Everything was fine. Same devotion—at the ashram or in the office, no difference. Then knowledge and devotion work together. If you know, then you will love God. If you love God, then only you will know. Then vichara and bhakti are the same.

I don't speak of bhakti because people are not prepared. In ego the heart is sold to someone else. Then what to surrender? What to give? With what can you love when it is sold to someone else?

***

A swami was telling me about the different states of samadhi, and I wondered what you thought. He said sahaj samadhi is the highest state.

The highest state is no-state.

Is that what you are established in?

[laughs and rolls his eyes] What can be said? Highest state is no-state—statelessness. Who has given name to this highest state? To give a name, somebody should be higher than

the highest state. Parents name the child because they were born earlier than the child. To give name to the highest state, there must be someone higher than that, and I don't know who that could be.

It is all creation of the mind. When there is no mind, there is no state. Your true nature is no-state. Remove all concepts and this will be your own state, whether you are walking, talking, eating, or sleeping.

When the breeze pays a visit to the fish market, the garden, and the cemetery, does it accept or reject anything? This stateless state is something like that.

From the side of bondage, there can be states. From bondage, the mind is not open to your own Self. The mind is not fully surrendered to the Supreme Power. There can be states and stages of ignorance or bondage, not wisdom.

If someone dies that you love, is sadness there? Do you have emotions in the stateless state?

Yes, when everyone is weeping for the departed soul, you weep with them. When they are dancing at the wedding, you dance with them. From here you can do everything because you know the reality. You are on the stage, and this part is given to you. This drama is given to you—so sometimes you are a king, and sometimes a slave. If you know you are the source, you can play any role and not be tainted.

So, if you just remember who you are—

No, not remembering. Remembering depends on memory. This is not that. A human being does not have to remember he is a human being. He does not confuse himself with a donkey. He knows very well he is a human being, without remembering. Introduce yourself to yourself, and there is no need for remembering.

If you can't do it yourself, approach someone with all humility, serve him, and ask how to be released from the suffering.

***

Why are so many people in delusion?

Because they don't open their eyes to the sun. It is not the sun's fault.

Is everyone free to do that?

Everyone is free to open their eyes. Shut your eyes now, and you won't see. Aren't you free to open your eyes? Most people don't open their eyes, and they don't see. It is your free will to open your eyes now.

I assume, because I am a part of everything, that there is no individual self here, that there is no individual freedom here. It is just happening. So am I free to open my eyes?

You are free. Freedom doesn't stop you from anything. But you must know, "Now I am opening the eyes." Everybody thinks, "My eyes are blind." Nobody is blind, just unfortunate.

So everybody is free?

Yes, but they don't feel they are free because they see a wall. This wall is desire. All desires belong to the past. So when you don't have any desires, your eyes are open. Try now, and tell me. Don't let desire stand between you and freedom, just for one second, and tell me.

There is nothing. Just emptiness.

That's it. So, who opened your eyes now? The cloud was desire. Any desire is a cloud.

The quickest method, the most direct method, meant only for a few very sharp people, is inquiry. Instantly you can be enlightened. All other methods will eventually lead you here.

In devotion there is duality between the devotee and the divine. Ultimately, the devotee has to surrender completely to the divine. If he surrenders completely, then he has no more business. Then the divine will look after him.

But nobody does this. Bhakti is love. It is romance. It can't be just going to the temple for an hour. It is a romance you can never forget for an instant. It's a real romance with your own Self. If you surrender to the divine, your work is done. Surrender or inquire. There are many other paths, like yoga and tantra, but I don't see any freedom resulting from them.

***

When I ask the question "Who am I?" it seems like a process or a practice.

Listen carefully. It is not that. When you ask this question "Who am I?" I am not taking you somewhere else. If I tell you even to take two steps somewhere, it may be a process. But if I tell you to stay wherever you are, you must be staying here. Is it a process?

Just see where this question arises from. Don't think about it; don't step out or go away somewhere or make any kind of effort. Just be conscious. Are you not conscious when you ask the question?

Yes.

Before the question arises, are you not conscious that there is no question in the mind?

Yes. But what is conscious of the—You didn't get it. Aren't you conscious of any question or any activity? Aren't you aware of whatever you are doing? When you are eating, you are aware of eating. If you are dancing, you are aware that you are dancing. And if you are not eating or dancing, aren't you also aware?

Yes.

This awareness is your Self. Whether you are doing anything or not, this awareness is your nature.

Yes, I know that.

You are not to know it! Knowing is something else. I am asking you to just be there.

This is called consciousness. Any activity or no activity, any sadhana or practice, starts from consciousness. And if you are conscious of consciousness within the consciousness, there is no problem, whatever you do. Nobody knows this, and so they suffer.

***

How is it possible to awaken without a method? So many people are doing practices—

The people who are not fit for Self-inquiry are not fit for the final assault. So they are attracted to yoga and other paths. That will, ultimately, lead to the same inquiry. Without this inquiry, there is no freedom. So everything else is a delay of freedom.

You see, with all practices, mind is involved. Whenever you practice, you make up your mind to practice, and you need body and mind. Inquiry is striking the root of the mind itself.

In practice, you are working with the mind. "I meditate," you say. This is the mind, the ego, that starts to meditate. For what and for whom?

In inquiry the root of the mind is challenged. When you say, "I am meditating," the meditator is never challenged. You fix a goal in the future to be gained from meditation. This goal in the future must be based on some idea in the past. So you are dipping in the past, not the present. You may attain that goal, but since it is not here before the practice, your practice is to get something not already here. Something is absent and you are striving to attain what is absent; thereby, you deny the presence of what is already present.

Whatever you gain you will lose again, because its nature is not eternal. Therefore, do not strive for things which are not now here. Instantly you can inquire, "Who is the one who is going to meditate, and what is the purpose of its meditation?" Before doing anything, you have to solve the problem yourself. Go sit quietly, and discover who is the meditator before doing any practice. Getting into practice without knowing who is practicing will not bring you the result of freedom and truth.

Inquiry is best to win freedom—here and now without any effort. In other practices you need effort; you need subject and object. The meditator becomes the subject, and freedom becomes objectified as the object. Freedom is not an object, it is the subject, and you have to start from the subject. The subject is free always. So why not start with the subject who is seeking for the freedom and inquire, "How am I chained and fettered?"

Where is the bondage? Maybe the bondage is a concept. You feel that you are bound, and you are bound. Then take another concept. "I am free" is a concept to overthrow the previous concept that "I am bound." Having done away with the previous concept of bondage, this one also falls away.

What's left? Emptiness! Freedom doesn't mean you have to win something. When you shun all notions and all ideations, you need not do anything, as freedom is not a notion. It is the birthright of every human being. This blessed incarnation is the final incarnation, if you desire freedom.

Otherwise, another round is waiting. Why another round? Because this is all imagination, and imagination is never-ending. A child sees a ghost in a room, and for the child, it is a ghost. The child is very afraid, but in truth, the ghost never existed.

***

You said that everybody you met has garbage, so I gave up hope.

But I said throw away the garbage. Did you do it?

No.

So you're right; there is no hope. Hope itself is garbage. Expectation is garbage. Expectation to become something else at a later date is a basket of garbage on your head. If you don't want to throw it away, if you like it, then keep it. We need someone to do this job also. Every city needs people to remove the garbage. Since I said throw away the garbage, and you have not thrown, you must like this profession.

I don't like it.

But you said there is no hope of throwing away the garbage. What does it mean? If you like garbage, you are garbage. You become what you think. If you think of garbage, you become garbage. At the time you are thinking garbage, at that time who are you? Who you should be? If you think of garbage at that time, what do you smell all around?

Garbage.

Garbage, yes. You will be so accustomed to garbage you will live in the garbage dump itself. You will not like to go out of the garbage. This manifestation is garbage. When you give rise to a thought, you invite garbage, and you must suffer. This thought is garbage. When you give rise, all the garbage is manifested suffering, and death manifests.

Don't give rise to a thought, and tell me. Don't just listen. This must be experienced. Don't give rise to this thought "I am so-and-so." Don't give rise to this thought *I,* and tell me where you are. Don't think; just do it, and tell me. Where now?

Nowhere.

In nowhere do you smell garbage?

No.

So stay there, in nowhere, and what is the problem here?

It's a problem that I can't find any difficulty.

Go deeper and tell me again. Look underneath. It is fathomless. Go down deeper and tell me. Don't think. Thinking is garbage. Go deeper. You said the problem is that there is no problem. Go deeper below this and see.

I'm free.

Free of problems and free of no problems.

So what have you done to be free? Look within yourself, and what do you see? Don't look here and there or nowhere. Then this look is no-look. This look is consciousness itself. Where there is no there and no here and no where, this is consciousness itself, from where everything arises and falls.

Everything arises and everything falls. And you are not touched. These manifestations, destructions, dissolutions—you are not touched, not affected in the least. This manifestation is a painting in the emptiness. Can you paint a picture in space? This is a picture, called manifestation, painted into the empty space.

So when you look within, this picture has never been painted. Nobody can ever paint a picture in empty space. You need some wall on which to paint, some canvas on which to paint, some screen on which to paint.

Become that screen and see this painting of manifestation. Actually nothing ever existed. Nothing is still existing. Nothing will exist. This is the ultimate truth, and just by losing *I*, it is realized.

What is the difficulty? You are not to go anywhere. Simply keep quiet and question, "Who am I? Where am I? What do I want?" And you will get the answer instantly.

Once you know, you cannot get out of it. Everywhere you move, you move in consciousness. Before, the levels were different, from unconsciousness to unconsciousness. You were getting lost.

Consciousness alone is, and nothing ever exists beyond this consciousness. Once having known it, you become one with consciousness. There is no subject and no object. There is no experience, and none experienced. This is called freedom from everything.

This is the moment, this instant, we are speaking about. I believe you are in the instant. If there is any problem, ask me.

I want you to enter directly into experience and not to understand intellectually. This intellect takes the form of what you think, and you may be cheated again. Everything that you think, that thought manifests.

Once upon a time, you had thought about it, and there it is! It will cease instantly, when you decide in this instant, "No more! Enough!"

This is great luck to have entered into this instant! Great luck!

Totally conscious is *I*. All this is *I*. All these *I*'s are within this *I*. This is total *I*, in which past and present and future appear.

***

Get rid of all notions, intentions, and desires. Between this and that, between the past and the future, inquire; you will fulfill your promise that "if I get a human form, I will get enlightened."

This incarnation as a human being is blessed. The only purpose of this life will be fulfilled if you are free. Otherwise, this miserable suffering will not end. This dress of a human form is meant only for freedom.

All the rest, you have enjoyed through other species. You have passed through 8.4 million species to sit in front of me. It is not difficult to be free. Freedom is within you. Love is within you, and you are searching at the supermarket. This samsara is a supermarket dealing in commodities. Turn your back on it and you are free. Return home.

The sun is so big, much bigger than the earth, yet a single cloud can hide the sun. Clouds are thoughts. Likewise, the *I*-thought is hiding the Self. The *I*-thought is hiding peace, beauty, and love. How to remove the cloud? Inquire, and it will vanish when you inquire, because it is not real.

***

Poonjaji, can you help me?

Well, let's see. You have been in Poona for fifteen years. Did you get what you want?

Well, I grew a lot.

Let us say that you went to a restaurant for a big meal. As you come out, a friend says, "Let's go to that other restaurant." Will you go?

No, I am already full.

So I ask you, "Are you full? Did you get what you want in Poona?"

No.

So what do you want?

Pure consciousness.

Very good. So how to get there? If you are at the office and you receive a phone call that your house is burning down, what would you do?

I would drive home right away.

Good. Along the way a friend says, "Let's go to a restaurant." What will you do?

I will go home.

Go home. Yes. Why? Because your house is on fire. You have to take care of the house first, right? You may not even eat that day, right? You might forget about lunch. You will forget about friends along the way. Like this, you come to me to see consciousness. Okay?

Good. Don't think of past or future. The past is a graveyard. It is the office, and you are rushing toward your house. If you don't think of the past, you can't think of the future either. To think of the future, you must stand in the past. So the past and the future are not in your mind. Mind itself is only past and future, so don't think now. Okay?

Just a few seconds. I want just a few seconds out of your life. Okay?

No thought, no past, no future. Now tell me, who are you? In this no-thinking, you are facing consciousness and consciousness is facing you. So tell me, who are you?

I am consciousness.

Yes, very good. Now look around, and what do you see?

I see emptiness everywhere.

Yes. Emptiness everywhere. Now, in emptiness, give rise to a thought. Any thought will do. From where does it come?

It comes from emptiness.

Very good. And what is it?

It is empty!

Yes. Now let it sink back into emptiness, and what happens?

It is like a bubble that starts to form and sinks back.

Yes. And what do you see?

Emptiness everywhere. Even thoughts, people—the world is empty.

Very good. And this realization?

Also empty!

CHOOSING TOTAL DEATH

I feel like I'm almost there, but it seems as if there is some death experience waiting. Is there a death experience?

As the raindrop falls from the sky, it is afraid. This falling is a transition period. The raindrop is afraid it will be lost. It will fall and be destroyed. But when it falls into the ocean, that fear dissolves because the raindrop has become the ocean itself.

Fear will come. There cannot be any explanation except that the troublesome ego is experiencing that it is dying. Due to our association for so many years with the ego, we believe that we are dying.

When we are really living, we are free. When touching eternity, this death experience is total death. In the world, everybody dies only to be reborn. So really, nobody is dying.

The possibility is the actual death of the ego, of ignorance. With that total death, ego will not be reborn again. You have become eternal. Total death is to never be reborn again!

When you become eternal, having gotten rid of this circle, that death is total death. There may be fear for some time, but then there is tremendous happiness also.

**

One day I was driving from Bangalore to my mining camp. I stopped to put some water in the radiator of my jeep. I went to a lake and there I saw a snake. It had caught hold of one leg of a frog. Meanwhile, some flies were coming near the frog, and the frog was eating the flies.

I was surprised. What to do? I could get a stick and free the frog. But the snake is living on the frog, and the frog is living on flies. So I am seeing the dharma in this situation.

If I remove the frog from the mouth of the snake, the snake will abuse me. The frog is already half dead and will be miserable all his life.

And I can't save the fly, so I thought it better to disappear from there and not interfere in the world order. Don't trouble any beings, and don't be troubled.

Like a frog, from the moment we are born, from the first day, we are in the mouth of death. Every minute she is sucking. The moment which is yesterday is already finished. This snake has already succeeded: one day out of our life gone.

We are enjoying other pleasures and diversions, not knowing our blood is in the mouth of the serpent which has not left anybody.

Remember it—one leg in the mouth of the serpent—and perhaps you will pay attention to something else. Only by knowing ourselves can we avoid this serpent called death. You will know then that you are not the body, and death takes only the body, not the indweller of the body; the indweller is eternal.

When you know who you are, death can't touch you. You won't mourn the death of this body any more than you mourn taking off your cardigan.

Millions of times you have already borne this death, so do it now for the last time.

Remove everything that you will eventually lose. Removing means not identifying with, not being attached to, anything that is perishable. It is no use trying to keep it. This life will go on very smoothly without a thought.

***

I have this fight inside myself. Each morning in line for satsang I feel this drive to push to get close to you. But then I tell myself, "No effort, no, no. Go back." I have to push and I have this fight inside myself.

When you don't push, you will see the force of pull.

I feel the strong pull.

For pulling you have to give up all your efforts, allow yourself to be pulled. If you enter a whirlpool in the river, do you need to push, or are you pulled into it? Who will push the boat into the whirlpool? It will be pulled in and down, and you will be forced to sink down into the whirlpool, never to come up again. This is the pull.

Throw away your oars. Break the mast! Allow your boat to be pulled into the flood of the whirlpool, and you keep quiet. The rest will be done.

I don't trust that it will happen if I don't do it.

This is happening by itself. You move toward the whirlpool; it is happening by itself. You don't need to make any effort. Keep quiet, and throw away everything you have. Throw away the oars and break the mast. Don't row any more. That's what you have to do.

It will be very smooth sailing. When you row you are fatigued, and sometimes accidents happen. With no oars, no rowing, there will be no accidents at all. Try. Don't row the boat. You will go along with the river.

***

What is the intellect, and is there such a thing as choice?

Choice is of the intellect. Intellect will tell you, "This is a mirage. Don't go for a swim in the desert sands. If it was not here in the morning, or the previous night, then it must be unreal." This is intellect.

A wrong choice is to choose to swim and quench your thirst in the mirage. Then you drink sand.

When you stay quiet and reason out that "it was not there before, so it is not real, and I won't try to swim there," this is called a very sharp intellect.

To make a very firm decision, that the sand is sand and the river is river, is a sharp intellect. Bring the mind, the intellect, and the breath back to the source, and the choice will be the right choice. Otherwise, no choice is going to be a very correct choice.

But can we really make a choice?

How does this choice arise? There was once a young prince who was sleeping with his wife on one side and his newborn son on the other.

I will show you the choice of this man 2,535 years ago. In the night he woke up and made a choice: "Let me have freedom."

Where does this choice come from? His father was there, happy in the kingdom. Other princes of the world were there, sleeping with their queens. All other kings, all other beings, are still sleeping with their queens. [*laughs*]

What about this choice? Where does this choice arise from?

From beyond.

Yes. From beyond. So go to the beyond. Your part of the job is to go to the beyond. And then it will take charge. It will conduct every routine of your life. This prince that I spoke about led a very beautiful life. Centuries have passed, and still we are getting inspiration from him. This is a choice.

***

Papaji, what is hell?

Hell is the mind turned outward and saying, "I am the body." This is hell, here and now. How can you have peace when the mind decides that the playing field is only the body? Nobody can have true peace. Every body is going to die.

What is heaven? The mind turned inward is heaven. As it is said in the Bible, "The kingdom of heaven is within." And how to win this kingdom of heaven? Surrender to awareness.

Awareness, Being, endlessness—this is called heaven, freedom, enlightenment. This is emancipation from the process one has been passing through for millions of years. The mind turned inward will, for the first time, see its own beauty, its own source, and will not turn back to that which is disturbing. Always you stay with what you love the most. There is no turning back from there.

It is your decision. "Now I have decided to win freedom, to have love, to have consciousness of Being itself. I want to have holiness for the first time." This decision is foremost. This is the only decision you have to make. Surrender to Being, awareness, and bliss.

Those who have decided, "I have to know myself. I have to return home," instantly will get it. This is the true dharma. This will return you to your own awareness.

Performing sadhanas, tapas, and practices to win freedom and enlightenment is what was done in the past. But we are here, and now you can get freedom instantly. It is new, but it is very true.

If you like something, you will surely fall in love instantly. It is a romance.

In one glance you will forget everything. One glance is enough.

The mind has to decide what is beautiful and what is ugly. The mind, wherever it travels, loves beauty, but does not really know what beauty is.

Once there was a Persian diamond merchant who came to sell diamonds to the Moghul kings of India. While on his way to their capital in Delhi, he passed through Punjab, where he came to the river Jalum.

He saw a very beautiful girl who came to fill a pot of water. They exchanged one look, and he followed her home. He discovered that she was the daughter of a potter.

He sat down under a tree and forgot about everything except the girl. He went again and again to the potter's house and bought pots. All he had to pay with were his diamonds. So he bought pots with diamonds. He went again and again just to see his love. He spent all of his diamonds.

Because he was a foreigner, her parents would not allow her to marry him. This man spent the rest of his life under that tree. He forgot his trade in India. He just stayed to see his beloved.

When you see that this is a trade, you will spend everything for what you want. This is beauty, awareness, love—your own Being. You are already spending all that you have, and for what?

Only check the outgoing tendency of the mind. This is your choice.

***

Everything will bow down before a strong decision. If you say, "I am going to do it, here and now!" what will happen? Heavens will shake. Gods will tremble and offer you everything.

***

This desire to be free has arisen in a very few people. Free in this life. This year. This month. Now. This desire will decide. Like a moth who falls in love with the flame and rushes toward it without any delay. No holding on or holding back along the way. How much time to become flame itself? Going toward the flame is the decision to be free—going toward the Atman.

The Atman consumes you, giving you eternal existence, eternal consciousness, and eternal bliss. And nobody knows it. Everyone is searching outside through the senses. Whatever you see, wherever you see name and form, it is not true. These names and forms will never give you peace or love. Whatever you see, feel, or experience through pleasurable sense objects ultimately will leave you hungry.

So this is the decision and the discernment. With this discernment, this discrimination, a few will decide, "I want to be free." They will find a teacher. The teacher is within you. The satguru is within you. Your desire for freedom is going toward that satguru, that Brahman.

***

First there must be nothing else on your mind. You must have no other desire or fascination that hinders your desire for freedom. Other desires compel you to again return to the cycle of birth and death. Finally, you decide to return with no hindrances, no preoccupations. Your decision is very strong. You are conscious of your decision, of where you are going. You are very conscious of what you have selected.

Now, for the first time, you are face-to-face with consciousness. If you have the slightest desire for anything else, you are showing your back. And this back means not less than thirty-five million years. You turned your back once, and now, thirty-five million years later, you are again near.

Facing toward That, this desire, this seeker of truth meets consciousness, satguru, face-to-face. Consciousness is now reflecting itself. Reflection of consciousness on this seeker, face-to-face. Reflection of this truth, this consciousness, is the seeker.

With this reflection, the desire is burned. Desire is gone. You have come with a desire for freedom. When you arrive at the goal, desire is gone. So who is left? Consciousness reflecting on its own consciousness. No difference between Brahman within you and without.

You have been searching from place to place and did not find it, because it is seated within you. Within all hearts. Here you did not search.

When you look within your own heart, this search is over. Here ends the journey. The cycle, the karma, the destiny, whatever it is, is over.

***

How is it that so few have arrived at this state?

Arrived? None have arrived. This is only talk along the way, before arriving. We are going toward freedom. We are going toward love. We are going toward the ocean.

But how many rivers do you see in the ocean? How many rivers are there after they meet the ocean? It is talk on the way.

Raindrops are falling on the ocean. As they fall, they create a friendship. "Where are we going? We are going together. We will all be together after we fall." Where is the rain or raindrops at the ocean? How many raindrops will survive the ocean?

All the experiences are along the way. Once you touch your own Self, what will you become?

This mind has created the whole universe. Millions of beings. As soon as the mind touches its own source, which is empty, how many emptinesses will be there in the emptiness?

All these questions are not wise. Only an ignorant man speaks about these things. Therefore, just keep quiet and see. Don't start a single thought from the ground of the mind.

On this question, I would like to speak to you.

What an understanding! I say, don't raise a single thought, and you say, on this topic you want to speak?

***

I want to be free, but—

But? You say "but"!? How much time do you really spend, in a day, on this desire?

About five minutes.

To be free of suffering, you must be attached to what does not separate you from bliss. First discern all the objects of the world, and tell me any object that brings you constant happiness. Any object that you like most.

If you have not found any object, then reject all objects. If some ass kicks you—and this ass represents the objects of the world—and you still follow it, you are acting like a donkey.

See it on the road. A donkey is pursuing an ass, and the ass kicks from behind. The donkey's nose is bleeding; its eyes are cut from the kick. What will you do?

Run away.

Yes, leave the ass. But I see the donkeys of this world getting kick after kick, bleeding from the nose, losing their teeth, and still they will not leave the ass. These donkeys I see every day. They come here also.

You spend twenty-three hours and fifty-five minutes getting kicks from the ass. And still you want to smell it. So what do you choose?

To leave it.

So if you reject this ass, where do you face?

I am faced toward myself.

Right! You have become wise. What is this ass? The whole universe is an ass. Everything from creation to destruction is an ass. You spend all your time getting kicked by this ass. Tell me, who is the man who has not been kicked by this ass? Everybody has been kicked, and still they are following for more.

To turn away from this ass for just five minutes, what does it mean? Any name and any form is an ass. Form means four legs and one tail behind. Turn your eyes from this ass of name and form. Twenty-three hours and fifty-five minutes of ass; turn your face and what happens?

I am free.

Excellent. You asked the question "How?" This is how. What did you do to find out if you are free? Did you think about it?

No, I experienced myself without any doubt.

Why not stay here? Are you not enjoying it? Isn't it reasonable to stay here always?

Very reasonable, without doubt.

Why not spend all the rest of your life engaged in this affair? "I am consciousness. I am bliss. I am existence." Speak to it. Think about it. When you meet sincere friends who are interested, speak to them from here about it. Spend all the rest of life involved in this affair, as long as your karma lasts.

Karma means merits or old tendencies now fructifying. This is what was responsible for you being given this body, and it has to last its time. It has to last. So let this time be spent with the love of your own Self.

HOW TO BE IN THE WORLD

Make the best use of this present time. Be reasonable, and understand.

I don't advise you to go to a cave. I don't advise you to live in communes or ashrams or monasteries. Live a happy life, a family life. Keep up your profession, as good boys, so the world is not troubled by you. All other stations of life depend on the station of the householder. Students, monks, old people, and sanyassins all depend on the earning of the householder. Why not help these people, instead of becoming a beggar yourself?

This idea of a monastery or commune is not a new concept. It is a Buddhist concept, and it has not paid off. No monastery has been successful at producing enlightenment. It has been tried; there are no shortcuts.

Traditionally, here in India, there are different stations of life. Student life, twenty-five years; householder life, twenty-five years. Then your children are grown up and you leave for the forest to seek enlightenment. In the fourth stage you are free to do what you like. Running away from life has never paid anybody.

I'm a doctor. Whom should I serve? Who has the greatest need?

Patients.

Poor people?

Patients need a doctor.

Any patient?

Any patient.

Whoever comes?

Whosoever comes. This would be enough for you to get enlightened. The divinity can appear to you in the patient itself. Don't see the weight of the purse before you see the patient. A patient is a patient, but the doctors are not behaving like that. It is good to be a good doctor. Children are suffering. The world is suffering. Why not help? Better to help than to go and become a monk.

I see that I still have doubts that it can be so simple. I expect big experiences and bliss, and I expect it to be—

Hard and difficult.

Yes.

So go to the Himalayas and hang by your feet. [*laughter*] All kinds of trainings are still being done, because it is easier to do them than to sit quietly.

You can stand on your head for an hour, or recite mantras and chant them for hours. All this is possible. The mind is deceiving you; the mind doesn't like to be quiet. The only way the mind can be beaten is not to give rise to a thought. Don't start a thought. So simple. The mind likes to engage in activities and exercises. When you are not active mentally, this is peace.

***

When you return home to your profession and your society, remember that I don't tell you to run away from life. There are no problems. You will accept everything. There is no otherness at all. You have been putting on glasses that have a different shade; these glasses you must remove. The eyes that you use to see must change. The rivers, mountains, and friends won't change, but you wear the glasses of wisdom now to see no otherness. No strangers. All your own Self.

This whole world is your own Self. So who is good and who is bad? That will depend on your direct experience, not what any book or person tells you. So dive right now, and have the experience—then judge for yourself.

Just this teaching without direct experience doesn't mean anything. And experience is not far away. You must first decide what is good for you. Then take immediate action, and see the result.

***

Take very good care of the body because this is the rarest gift that nature can give you—a human birth. Take very good care of it, because it is a temple of God. God is seated in your heart. And this body will be useful to you for higher attainment of knowledge. Therefore, respect this body. Don't ignore it. Keep it very well and fit up to a complete human span of life.

***

I have no wife or family, and I am finished with all doing in the world. Can I stay and serve you?

If you don't know yourself, what help can you be to another? It will be the blind leading the blind. If you know yourself, you will help the world. This is the only help you can give to others. First know yourself; then have peace and happiness; then let others know how to have peace and happiness. You can't give this message until you have it yourself. Find yourself, the treasure, and then distribute it. It is an infinite treasure, and the more you give, the more it will multiply.

***

There once was a king who, after his daily prayers, would give the next person he saw anything he desired. One day a fakir was waiting while the king prayed. When the king finished, the fakir said, "I came to beg from you, but I see you are also a beggar. You are begging from God. So I will not beg from a beggar. I will beg from the same one you do."

Everyone is begging. Who is not a beggar? If you don't ask for anything, you will be given everything. If you don't ask anything, God will follow behind you. Everything will be added unto you, and you need not beg.

***

How can I be free from the things that keep me from being more compassionate? How can I be free from the limitation that keeps me from being more compassionate?

You want to be compassionate for other people? What is this precious gift you have that you want to give others so they will be happy? Can you give enough food for the starving half of the world? Once? Lunch or dinner? Can you give just one meal to the starving of this world?

No.

No. Then what do you want to give them? First food, then clothing, then shelter—isn't it? There you have nothing to give. So, perhaps peace of mind.

The world still can't feed these people. The richest countries have tried, and they cannot even feed and clothe and house the people of their own country, let alone others. So what will you do? Can you give peace of mind? Do you have peace of mind?

No.

Then how can you help others? This is a missionary concept: to want to go and help other people. We have all seen the missionaries who come to the underdeveloped countries.

I have seen the missionaries, trained in the postures of how to be "compassionate." They learned how to hold their hands, how to make their eyes moist. I have seen missionary dramas where all this is taught as a ritual. Compassion, as it is taught, is a political stunt and a religious falsehood. Compassion must be from the heart.

How to get it?

Find out who wants peace. Who wants to be compassionate? Introduce yourself to That which is compassion itself. Introduce yourself to That. Wherever it is. Turn your mind toward That and tell me. It may be nowhere. Tell me.

***

What is the responsibility after awakening?

First of all, this is not a good question. After awakening you will see everything very clearly, without knowing about it beforehand.

After enlightenment there is no ego and no doership. You will abide in something else. One has to first win freedom; then it will take care of itself.

This question is from the doer who wants to do something according to the rules of conduct. The awakened man responds spontaneously to the circumstances, and thus does not leave any footprints in the memory. This is just like a bird flying in the sky, leaving no trace behind.

A post-enlightenment question cannot be asked in pre-enlightenment. First win enlightenment. Then see if you can ask this question. There is nothing to do, and nothing to not do. Only be spontaneous in the circumstances. When the mind is dead, there can be no concepts of action.

It is for the Self, not the mind, to act. The mind and the ego can make mistakes, not the Self. You merge into

Self after freedom. This is the end of all problems, conducts, and moralities. That situation cannot be described or imagined or touched.

***

You say in freedom there are no concepts. Yet, if you work in a hospital, the hospitals are filled with concepts. How do you reconcile these two?

When the ego is there with the thought "I am doing this, I am doing that, I want this, I don't want that," then there is trouble, and there are mistakes also.

When you recognize yourself—as when a river discharges into the ocean and is no longer a river—all qualities are gone. Ocean has no limits. When you are free you are no longer a man with past habits. You are not functioning, because doer is not there; mind is not there.

No mind is functioning, so who is? The lord within is functioning through the person, for the good of others. Otherwise, it is no use.

After enlightenment your work is done. When you are free, freedom takes charges of you. Something else will arise instead of ego, instead of doer. *I am doing* will no longer be there.

Another power called prajna, transcendental function, will take charge of you. It will enter into all your nerves, and all the atoms of your body will be changed. You will no longer be the previous person.

You need not make any effort. Simply surrender to the lord seated in your heart. Then you will see how beautiful this lifespan—in dealing with people, your relationships—how beautiful it will become.

Action will not come from ego, but from that supreme Purusha [enlightened intelligence]. It will be in charge. Whenever you speak, it is speaking. Whatever you see, it is seeing. Your eyes will be changed. There will be no hatred; these eyes will see God everywhere.

That difference will suddenly take place if you surrender. If you adore, and see only God seated in the emptiness of your heart, all will be done.

Here, if you want to see the prime minister directly, you can't see him. You have to approach him through so many ministers and recommendations. They will tell you he is very busy. You even have to salute the security guards at the gate. You will not be allowed to enter to see the prime minister.

But somehow, if you have befriended the prime minister, he will go, himself, to the airport to see you. So you have to make friends with the lord of this universe, not with the guards!

Don't miss this key, and you will not suffer, even at the time of the great departure—even the Creator has to face this departure. Everyone is miserable in the face of this departure: to give up everything that has been held to, to leave friends, to turn away from all manifestation.

Yama, Lord of Death, is in front of you. Everyone must face it. Millions of times you have faced it, and that is why you are afraid of death: because you had death experiences many times before. Fear of death is only this. Everyone is afraid of death. But when you have done it, and won this deathlessness before death, if the god of death comes, you will recognize him and you will hug him. You will kiss death as none other than your old friend.

When suffering arises in your mind, simply question, "Who is suffering?" That's all. Why does suffering leave with this question? Because you have separated yourself from the situation. Ask the question "Who is bound?" and you will discover no chains or fetters.

***

If I don't do anything, how will anything get done?

When you make an effort in dealing with things, you need some power. You need some power even to raise your mind. Effort can be made physically or mentally.

What enables you to make an effort? You say, "I want to go from here to there!" You need effort to walk. Legs are there. The mind is there. The destination is in your mind and the road is there to travel. Where do you get the effort to lift a step? What enables the foot to walk and the mind to mentate?

I don't know.

You only know what has been known. You do not know that unknown through which this known is known. When you say, "I do not know," where do you go?

I asked the mind.

The mind said, "I do not know," not the foot. Ask the mind where it gets its power to think.

It is desire.

Desire and mind are the same thing. Where does the desire arise from to become a desire?

I don't know.

The power comes from nothing. Your effort arises from nothingness. When you walk, the power is from nothingness. [*long silence*]

Freedom is timeless!

Yes. Anything more?

There is no distance to travel.

Yes. Carry on.

I don't understand why I haven't understood this before, and I am filled with wonder at life and that there is no separation. [laughs] And I am very happy.

I bow down before that happiness.

***

I have a five-year-old son. How do you work with a five-year-old mind?

You have to stop thinking. Children are not behaving well because parents are not well-behaved. If the mother is wise, without thought, she will see the divine in her children. She will worship the child as God itself. She will see her own reflection in the child, her own Self in another form. You will be a real mother if you are realized.

***

I am a therapist and—

A therapist? [*laughter*]

And I wonder how it will be when I go back.

You will be a better therapist and you will help many people. Then you will finally know what you are speaking about. This is compassion. Simply your touch, your sight, will work. You will know a different way of therapy. You will work more efficiently, with compassion.

Before it was a profession. Now it will be a compassion. You will have good luck wherever you go. Wherever you are, you are here. Wherever you will be, you'll be here. Go wherever you like; this is all your domain. Wherever you will be, you will be in consciousness. Consciousness is your abode. Consciousness is happiness, peace.

So work in happiness and peace. Teach all your friends the way to be happy. As you received happiness, give them this simple secret now—to be happy.

Do whatever you want. It will work itself, by itself, within itself. That pride, that ego, will no longer be there. Now, working will happen in a very different way, where work is no longer work dictated by mind or ego. Very spontaneous work with other people. Very natural, coming from Self to Self. This change you will experience yourself. I wish you the best of luck.

***

Someone asked if it is possible to lose it. I know you can never lose it.

You say you can never lose it. I say, "Now vigilance."

I will tell you about my own experience. In 1947, I was walking in front of this post office, going to Lardbar. I was on the safe left-hand side. A Ford car with a running board hit me from behind.

People gathered around and they told me, "Look what happened. We took the license number of the car. You must be hurt."

So I rolled up my pants leg, and the pants were torn, of course, but there was very little hurt to the body. A little scratch. And there was the running board next to me. They said, "Let's go to the police station." I said nothing. I was not interested.

What is this kind of vigilance?

Great stress is given that you must be very vigilant. So what is this kind of vigilance? It's not vigilance concerning the body at all! Who was protecting this body?

On another occasion I was coming from South Mangalore to Bangalore, a distance of about six hundred miles by car. I had just loaded a ship to Rotterdam. After loading the shipment of iron ore to Rotterdam, I got the manifest from the captain.

By this time I was very tired. The unloading was offshore, so I had to go to the sea and then spend eight hours with the captain, getting the paperwork finished.

It was very warm and I was very fatigued, but still I needed to get back to Mangalore. So I got into my jeep. I had to travel from sea level to five thousand meters in altitude in seven very sharp hairpin turns.

I was very sleepy. I thought I should pull over, but then I thought, "Well, it's only eight miles to the other side, where I can get a cup of coffee and some rest. Here, there are wild elephants, and they could roll the jeep into the valley. So, only half an hour more."

I fell asleep. I slept on the steering wheel itself. When I arrived on the other side, I had passed over a very difficult, narrow one-way track along the edge of a valley one kilometer deep. The hill was one kilometer up.

On the other side, I was very fresh. I had a full sleep, and awoke with my head on the steering wheel, still going down the road. Now I was refreshed, so I kept driving another five hundred kilometers after that.

The question is: If I was sleeping, who was driving? I cannot find the answer. But you are here now; you are in the experience—you must understand this.

I was speaking of vigilance. There are very few people who get it. Vigilance is not manipulation. It is interest in where the word is becoming a word.

Well, I would like to share an experience of when I was driving in my car—

No, no, you don't understand. [*laughs*]

***

Once a truly empty man lay down for a short nap under a tree. When he awoke, he stood up and picked up his belongings and begging bowl. He saw many beings sitting around him. They all stood up and said, "Thank you for satsang."

"But I didn't speak a word to you. I was sleeping."

"Yes, sir. This satsang we cannot get in heaven. We are all gods of different heavens, and we have to come here to have your satsang. This satsang is not happening, even in the heavens."

"We are very busy and chattering all day. So much fun there. So much fun. Enjoyment that humans can't even think of. We were very busy in our enjoyments. We wanted some peace. We looked around, searching for where we could have some peace of mind."

The gods from the heavens looked around, and on the earth, they found this man who was sleeping. A man with no thoughts in the mind is emitting rays of peace and love! Everyone is attracted to the person who has no concept in the mind.

"So we have come because here is the place of love and peace. Thank you for this satsang."

As they returned to their abode, they showered flowers on this man, and the tree also came into bloom and dropped flowers on him.

Just keep quiet and see what happens. All nature will love you. You will be better taken care of than by your own mother who gave birth to you and put you in all this trouble.

But this other mother—consciousness, if you know that she is your original mother—she will take care of you and give you peace and happiness and deathlessness also. No other mother can give you this. Deathlessness in eternity. This mother we do not recognize, and we get into trouble.

When you love, you love all beings. When you eat, everybody is eating off your plate, even the beings who have died and the ones who are yet to be. When you see, all the eyes collected together are seeing through this retina.

***

What is the purpose of life?

Responsibility to the society. First know your own Self; then serve all other beings as your own Self.

That will arise naturally in me?

No. You are not involved in that. You are not in the picture at all. When the doer is here, it is ego. When the doer surrenders to the Supreme Power, it is finished. Then the Supreme Power itself will arise and function in this body.

You will see this—know your own Self first; then surrender to that power. Then intuition will take charge of you, and it will function through your mind and brain. Then you will be able to function a million times better than as an individual ego. Not "manpower," as they say, but divine power.

Is there anything I can do for you?

Yes, why not?

What?

Help others. But not on anybody's behalf, not mine nor your own. Help whoever comes.

***

I am very much interested in this message of peace. It has to be given in silence. No clash with anyone. Sit quiet, even in your house. This will work better than the statements of the world premiers. Send a message of peace from within the heart, in silence, to all beings in this world.

That is what I desire, nothing more. I am not interested in any ashram. If I haven't done it yet, and I am eighty-two, I will not start now. People even offered me islands they had purchased. I was never tempted. I am used to going from door to door, until the last few years, when physical problems kept me here. I have given you the trouble to come. I hope you don't mind.

***

Wherever there is truth, there must be the smoke of demons also. So be aware, because the jagnas of the rishis have been spoiled by the demons. This has been going on since the beginning. You needn't mind. Truth is our sentry now. You hold truth responsible.

There are hurdles. Whenever truth is spoken, the world becomes your enemy. What was wrong with Christ? He only spoke the truth. That was his sin, and he was put on the cross.

Speak the truth and you are hanged, burned, crucified—and you are happy. Look at Socrates. This Greek had lived a beautiful life, and he was given a cup of poison. Plato and others tried to save him, saying, "Master, we have bribed the policemen. In the night you come with us."

Socrates said, "No, my dear children, that is not going to happen. I have spoken truth all my life. I prefer death to living in a wrong way."

This is called truth. How long can falsehood survive? Keep truth, and finally truth will help you. You may be in trouble for some time. Christ was crucified. And how many benefited?

You have seventy or eighty years—why live a foolish way of life? Why not have a few years of wisdom instead of one hundred years of a foolish, stupid, wicked life? The language of peace is *mounam,* which means "silence." When you are in peace, happiness, and love, there is only one language you can speak, and it is silence.

THE ROMANCE OF LOVE: THE HIDDEN SECRET

They call it peace. They call it happiness. They call it love. They call it beauty. Still, it is untouched. It is much more beyond this. Whosoever has gone here has merged into it. No communication. No mind. No intellect. No senses. And this is the happiness. When these things cease, only then will you see the face of happiness.

***

Osho told me that love is God. But I am upset because I feel that only when *I* disappears will love be here.

Yes! That's it! That is really it. [*laughter*]

When you disappear, then love is here. Otherwise, instead of god of love, what is there is god of vasanas, god of desires, god of lust.

When the mind and the intellect disappear, then there will be love eternal. No beloved and no lover. Love alone. This is peace. Shanti. Being. Awareness. This is called love, beauty, bliss.

No better enjoyment than this for itself. No enjoyer and no enjoyed. This is joy, without any reason.

Disappear for one second, and see what happens. Just for one second, disappear. Just disappear for one second and see what it is.

Then you will fall in love with your own Self, for the first time in thirty-five million years.

***

When I am in nature, I am fine, or when I am with like-minded people. But I'm afraid that when I leave here, I will go back to old habits of the mind.

You must always concentrate your attention on the center of your heart. Then your daily activity has nothing to do with your inner inquiry. Just like a man who has TB: he may go to a movie or have lunch with a friend, but does he ever forget he is a TB patient? Keep your mind engaged on freedom. This must be your sole occupation throughout life. You don't just sit for one hour in meditation. How about the other twenty-three hours? It must be twenty-four hours—aware. Walking, eating, sleeping—this is a romance with your own Self.

I feel that romance.

Don't ever betray your beloved, or it is not true romance.

There was a prince who saw his beloved everywhere. He kissed the trees, the dog, and loved the birds and people, until finally he forgot the beloved and became the beloved. That is the romance. In true romance, no lover and no beloved—only romance. No subject, no object. Just love. Only love. This is romance.

***

I have a desire to drown in the sea of consciousness.

This is just like the fish in the ocean crying, "I am thirsty." Once you taste it, have a glimpse of it, you are already in That. So this consciousness becomes a playground. All of manifestation and beyond. Millions of planets are your playground. This desire to drown in a sea of consciousness is to dance from planet to planet. Let this desire continue. I don't mind. It is a dance, you see. You will never be out of step.

Instantly, when you speak of consciousness, you are in it. There is no separation. Then this desire is an eternal dance. And this greed for the further investigation into the fathomlessness of consciousness is not a desire. It is something else. Because it is limitlessness, the more you desire, the more that is there!

This doesn't come in the category of desire for objects. This is very, very intimate. Between two intimate friends. Between lover and beloved. Nobody else can taste it, or imagine what is happening between consciousness and her lover. This is the cosmic dance.

Continue with this desire, and it is no problem. This is between you and her. Never-ending desire. In all other spheres, the desire ends and you climb to something else. Not this. This may be a desire from the other side, and you are being pulled in response to that attraction.

***

I feel such strong heat. Strong burning fire. What is it?

All the store that you have accumulated and collected with great care and much interest—you have put a match to it and burned it. Now enjoy.

This is a fire that burns all karmas so you won't have to appear again in this suffering. You have seen your own cremation. All the karmas are finished. This burning is the fire of knowledge. The ego, mind, senses, and pleasures are all burned and over. Everything is over. This is called fire.

It is a very lucky person who will see his own cremation while alive. And he is putting fuel into the fire until the corpse is completely burned. And then he will dance! This is called Shiva's dance. He has won. Everything is finished. No more notions or thoughts or desires. All ended in the fire. And then happiness will come and you will dance the eternal dance.

***

You can't escape love. Once you touch it you get lost. Nothing ever exists that can come out again.

Everything is discharged and becomes That itself. When the river enters the ocean, it does not return.

The river entering the ocean asks, "Will I always be like this?" What a joke!

The wave is afraid: "I want to forever remain a wave." The fear in the mind of the wave is, "I will be lost!" Where will it go? Even if it is lost, where can it go and what will it become?

When the wave form is lost, it returns to its source. Ocean she was; ocean she is; ocean she will be. There is no time concept at all. Time is only in the mind of an ignorant person. In light and wisdom there is no such notion that "I am separate." All is unity, love, and beauty. There is no escape. Ignorance is gone. This is eternal life. This is nectar.

Even though you are That itself, still some undercurrent is working: to be more, moving closer to love itself. That I cannot describe unless someone has had that experience and can agree that there is no end to it. If it is fathomless, this love process is also fathomless. It is never-ending. It will go on increasing, like an undercurrent. Like the river discharging into the ocean.

Some say, "All is over. You don't need to do anything more. And there is no further experience."

But I feel there is still movement, because it is fathomless, fathomlessness.

***

Whoever has gone into the kingdom has not returned, nor even sent a fax. No return, no information, and no description. You dissolve, and then you get this kingdom: eternal love, eternal Being, awareness, bliss. Who can say anything about it?

Being means that you dissolve every notion or ideation that you had about this kingdom. Whatever intention that you had about this kingdom is dissolved. That is your kingdom, from where there is no return.

No sun has ever shone there, no moon and no stars, no fire—such is that kingdom. Such is the location. And that location is the goal of everybody. And that location is here, now.

***

To give rise to the desire for freedom is itself a blessing on your land, your country, your family. The rest is for you to bless your own Self, and this can be done instantly. Don't entertain any kind of fear. Only sit quietly and keep quiet. This quietness is your nature. It will bring you home. Simply keep quiet. How difficult is it to keep quiet? You are not to give rise to any desire for anything.

The teacher will give you teaching only to the extent that you can absorb, then send you away and see what happens. Leaving body, mind, ego, senses, and intellect, have a firm conviction: "I am existence, consciousness, bliss." Don't figure it out. You have tried that before, and you know it is not successful.

You have to merge into existence and become one. Then dive into consciousness, and become one with consciousness. And then dive into bliss.

Up to this, the teacher can teach. Everyone is satisfied when they reach here, but there is more. There is another part of the teaching which is so sacred, so secret, so sacredly secret. The key of this secret is with whom? Nobody knows.

But I can say definitely that there is yet another secret. No one has asked. I have never heard of anyone going beyond and asking.

Here ends the matter. Really there is no end. It is fathomlessness. No one has measured the depth. The depth of the ocean has been measured; the depth of the sky, the depth of the planet, the limitation of the solar system have been measured. But this is not measured so far.

The more you go, the more you like to know.

***

People say that this transcendental experience cannot be described. But this is what I want to hear. Speaking from the yonder shore, describing the indescribable. From the silence, I want to hear some word that has not yet been conveyed.

People say it is beyond words. But still, I am in love with this description.

So far, I have not been successful in satisfying this, but you are young: you can help me.

GLOSSARY

Adharma: Anti-dharma.
Advaita: Teaching of non-duality.
Advaitan: Follower of Advaita teaching (non-duality).
Ananda: Pure conceptionless bliss.
Atman: Individuated consciousness, which is no different from absolute consciousness (Brahman).
Avadhuta: A self-realized saint living outside society's customs.
Bhakta: Devotee.
Bhakti: Devotion.
Bhiksha: Offering of food to the guru.
Bodhisattva: A being whose life is dedicated to the enlightenment of all beings.
Brahman: The absolute.
Chitdarman: Wish-fulfilling gem.
Darshan: Grace of the Self.
Dharma: Truth, path.
Dhyana: No-mind meditation.
Jnani: An enlightened one who knows through direct experience.
Kalpas: Cosmic circle of time. Four 5,000-year cycles equal one kalpa.

Kirta: Devotional service.
Leela: The divine play of the Self.
Mahatma: Title of respect.
Mahesh: Another name for Shiva.
Maya: Illusory world.
Prajna, pragna: Wisdom, consciousness.
Puja: Ritual of devotion.
Rishi: An enlightened sage.
Sadhana: Spiritual practice.
Sadhu: Wandering ascetic.
Sahaj samadhi: Natural absorption in emptiness while apparently engaged in the world.
Samadhi: Absorption in bliss.
Samsara: The bondage of suffering on the wheel of incarnation.
Samskara: Past tendency; impression created by previous desires, thoughts, and actions.
Sanyassin: Someone who has taken vows of renunciation and has left all worldly pursuits.
Satguru: The true teacher: no different from your own self; the transmitter of enlightenment.
Satsang: Association with Truth (sat: truth, sang: community).
Sattvic: Pure, clear.

Shakti: Divine energy.

Shanti: Peace.

Siddha: One who possesses yogic power.

Siddhi: Yogic power.

Sutras: Enlightened scripture.

Tapas: The burning of ignorance resulting from the unmoving commitment to Truth.

Vasana: Latent tendency, repressed subconscious identification.

Vichara: Self-inquiry.

ABOUT THE EDITOR

Eli Jaxon-Bear's eighteen-year spiritual search through Zen, Tibetan Buddhism, and other traditions ended when he knocked on the door of Sri Poonjaji's home in January 1990. Finding the Master alone in his bedroom, he was invited to sit on the bed, and the transmission began. He could not believe his good luck to be alone with a fully Self-realized Satguru. For the next three days, they were inseparable, eating their meals together, going to the market, and taking long walks. As seekers arrived to receive the teaching and transmission, Eli began taking notes after the meetings and, in preparation for this book, discussing his notes and the meetings with the man he called Papaji. When asked to go and teach, after Papaji tested his realization, Eli at first refused, saying that his wife, Gangaji, was the true satguru. He brought her to meet the master the following month. Gangaji has written the foreword to this book. Eli's other books include *Sudden Awakening: Into*

Direct Realization and *The Enneagram of Liberation: From Fixation to Freedom.* In 1995, after two refusals, he followed his teacher's written directive to teach, and he continues to meet with people around the world.

ABOUT SOUNDS TRUE

Sounds True was founded in 1985 with a clear vision: to disseminate spiritual wisdom. Located in Boulder, Colorado, Sounds True publishes teaching programs that are designed to educate, uplift, and inspire. We work with many of the leading spiritual teachers, thinkers, healers, and visionary artists of our time.

To receive a free catalog of tools and teachings for personal and spiritual transformation, please visit www.soundstrue.com, call toll-free 800-333-9185, or write to us at the address below. (Image I)

SOUNDS TRUE
PO Box 8010
Boulder, Colorado 80306

Image I

FRONT COVER FLAP

H.W.L. Poonja—affectionately known as Papaji—was only nine years old when he experienced his first samadhi, an altered state of consciousness where observer and object merge. As an adult, he sat in devotion with Sri Ramana Maharshi, and went on to become a master teacher in his own right, whose followers trekked across the world to sit in his presence.

Wake Up and Roar is a collector's edition of teachings delivered throughout his life, edited by Eli Jaxon-Bear, a longtime student of Papaji. Originally published in two volumes, here is Papaji's landmark work bound in one elegant book with previously unreleased photographs and a new foreword from Gangaji, his best-known student.

Presented in a question-and-answer format, *Wake Up and Roar* offers you an opportunity to awaken, here and now, regardless of background, practice, or personal circumstance. "The Self contains everything," teaches Papaji. "There is nothing apart from it. This is why you can call it emptiness. There is nothing beyond emptiness."

Blending humor, logic, and eye-opening storytelling, Papaji extends a gracious wisdom that speaks to the earnest seeker investigating the nature of mind, enlightenment, and "how to be in the world." In *Wake up and Roar,* he brings comfort and encouragement to practitioners from all traditions, at any stage of their inquiry into awakening.

BACK COVER FLAP

H.W.L. POONJA

(1910–1997) ... became a devotee of Sri Ramana Maharshi in 1944. He worked, held *satsangs,* and supported the many members of his extended family until his retirement in 1966. Papaji lived in Lucknow, India, where he received visitors from around the world. Many of his students are now sought-after teachers themselves, including Gangaji.

BACK COVER MATERIAL

LET ME TELL YOU A STORY

...A TEAM OF MOUNTAIN CLIMBERS WAS SCALING MOUNT EVEREST AND THEY CAMPED BELOW THE SUMMIT. ANOTHER TEAM WAS RETURNING FROM THE TOP AND SAW THEM CAMPED THERE.

"WHY ARE YOU CAMPED?" THEY WANTED TO KNOW.

"WE ARE WAITING FOR OUR MAP," THEY REPLIED. "WE FORGOT OUR MAP AT THE BASE CAMP AND WE HAVE SENT A SHERPA BACK TO RETRIEVE IT. SO WE ARE WAITING."

"BUT FROM HERE YOU DO NOT NEED A MAP!" THE RETURNING TEAM REPLIED. "THERE ARE NO AVALANCHES, NO PROBLEMS. FROM HERE, GO STRAIGHT TO THE TOP! NO MAP IS NECESSARY."

SO DROP ALL YOUR MAPS AND BAGGAGE. GO DIRECTLY TO THE SUMMIT FROM HERE.

—From *Wake Up and Roar*

www.ingramcontent.com/pod-product-compliance
Lightning Source LLC
Chambersburg PA
CBHW052048290426
44111CB00011B/1664